DRAWING by SEEING

DRAWING by SEEING

A new development in the teaching of the visual arts through the training of perception

by

HOYT L. SHERMAN

Professor of Fine Arts
The Ohio State University

with the collaboration of

ROSS L. MOONEY

and

GLENN A. FRY

❧

HINDS, HAYDEN & ELDREDGE
NEW YORK   PHILADELPHIA

ACKNOWLEDGMENTS

In the writing of this book and in the experimental work on which it is based, the author has depended upon the services of a number of persons on the staff of the Ohio State University. He is especially indebted to Dr. Ross L. Mooney of the Bureau of Educational Research for his services in the writing of the manuscript. Putting into verbal form ideas which are essentially graphic and dynamic in character is a difficult task.

Dr. Glenn A. Fry, Director of the School of Optometry, devised the extensive visual testing equipment and supervised the testing program. In this work, Dr. Fry took a keen personal interest and freely gave many hours of his time. The success of the project depended to a critical degree upon his contributions.

The project was supported, in all its research phases, by Dr. Arthur J. Klein, Dean of the College of Education, and Dr. Thomas C. Holy, Director of the Bureau of Educational Research. Through the College, the Bureau actively sponsored the program, appointed an advisory committee to assist in setting up the research procedures, and carefully evaluated the first draft of the report. The advisory committee was composed of Dr. Floyd C. Dockeray, Department of Psychology; Dr. Glenn A. Fry, School of Optometry; Mr. James R. Hopkins, School of Fine and Applied Arts; Mr. Louis H. Diercks, Department of Music; Dr. Robert Y. Walker, Department of Psychology; Dr. Louis E. Raths, Bureau of Educational Research; Mr. Robert E. Monroe, Department of Romance Languages; and Dr. Horace B. English, Department of Psychology, Chairman. Without this committee, the interest of the College, and the Bureau, there could not have been an experimental project for testing the central theory of the book.

Contributing in a hundred ways, both small and large, were colleagues in the School of Fine and Applied Arts and staff members in many other departments of the University. Thrilling, always, was the delightful company and support of the students in the experimental groups.

This book is truly the product of co-operative effort and a testament to the necessity for and potentiality of research work done in the co-operative manner.

HOYT L. SHERMAN

January 1, 1947
The Ohio State University,
Columbus, Ohio

CONTENTS

LIST OF FIGURES

Chapter One
INTRODUCTION

THIS BOOK describes some recent developments in the teaching of beginning drawing and painting. Results have been unusual in several respects, particularly in the quality of the drawings and paintings produced and in the rapidity with which beginning students have learned basic elements. Several novel methods are used: the work is done in complete darkness so that students do not see what they are drawing; models are abstract patterns projected on a screen by lantern slides; verbal instruction on how to draw and paint is carefully avoided; music is played throughout the drawing period.

The uniqueness of these methods calls for an explanation of the point of view from which they evolved. Without an understanding of the point of view, the procedures would appear bizarre and would be open to misuse and misinterpretation. The first part of the book is, therefore, given to a story of how the point of view developed and what it means when applied to the teaching program. With these matters as background, a description of actual procedures used in the classroom is given, followed by a report of the results obtained with experimental groups. The book concludes with a discussion of the manifold implications for art education and for other fields in which visual and creative abilities are required.

We began work on the problem of teaching beginning drawing some fifteen years ago. In search of essential ingredients for the training program, we first studied the qualities which seem to identify works of art as "great." In common with many other investigators of the subject, we concluded that the chief element is the degree to which drawings and paintings achieve a satisfactory pictorial organization. The problem then turned to an analysis of the elements which contribute to satisfactory pictorial organization and of the ways in which artists work in order to get these desired qualities in their paintings.

As this phase of the project developed, we became convinced that, underlying pictorial organization, there was a key idea which had not as yet been clarified, and that if it could be clarified, great improvements in the teaching of art might be possible, and the relation of art to other phases of modern life might be made more apparent. Hun-

1

dreds of drawings and paintings were analyzed until the search for the essence of pictorial organization became a habit of mind and a personal curse. Since consideration of the products of art alone yielded little light, the processes which artists used in coming to a satisfactory pictorial organization were studied. This investigation led us to the writings of artists who had described how they had performed the creative act. These writings were full of figures of speech, more tantalizing than revealing.

In 1938, however, some selection began to take place. As art products, the works of Masaccio, Rembrandt, and Cézanne seemed to possess most clearly a substantial and highly developed pictorial organization. As evidence on the process by which the creative act was achieved, the writings of and about Cézanne offered the most cues. These materials were chosen for intensive study.

While we were musing over passages in which Cézanne said that "painting is optics," that "in an orange, an apple, a sphere, a head there is a focal point," and that "the edges of these objects recede toward a point," our basic concept crystallized. Cézanne seemed to be explaining that drawing depends upon seeing and upon seeing in such a way that all points in a motif are related to a focal point.

We then conceived the idea that the degree to which one succeeds in getting unity in his drawing significantly depends upon the degree to which he succeeds in getting unity in his seeing. Teaching students to draw with satisfactory pictorial organization is to a major degree a process of teaching them to see with perceptual unity—that is, to see all points in a motif with relation to a focal point. The artist needs to be able to see the whole field at which he is looking and to see it in such a way as to place the parts in the whole through referral of the parts to a focal point.

This concept, if substantiated and used as a guide to the development of teaching, would sharply alter traditional methods of teaching drawing and painting: traditional methods are involved almost exclusively with a series of manipulative acts. The function of the eyes is neglected, and the training of the student in particular ways of seeing is lacking.

Before undertaking so radical a departure in teaching methods, we were constrained to test the hypothesis by referring it to our analyses of the pictorial organization of leading painters in the western tradition. If the hypothesis were successful in explaining satisfactory organization, each of the paintings and drawings which we had previously selected as "good" should show a focal point in relation to which other points in the picture would be oriented and related. Works considered "poor" would not have this type of organization.

Several hundred drawings and paintings were reviewed with this criterion in mind, and the hypothesis worked well. Indeed, it not only worked to select the good from the bad, but it also provided, for the first time in the writer's experience, a rationale in terms of which the whole problem of pictorial organization could be illuminated.[1]

This test, however, had two serious limitations: it was a personal evaluation, and it was limited to but one-half of the entire problem. The real test would come in teaching students to see with perceptual unity and then in determining the degree to which this training increased their drawing facility.

This then became the next venture in the project. The immediate problem was that of teaching students to see with perceptual unity. How could it be done?

Here a story about Rembrandt, apparently fabricated by Van Loon, provided a clue.[2] As a boy, Rembrandt happened one day to see, in suddenly exposed flashes, a cage of rats suspended from a rafter in his father's windmill. The sunlight falling on the suspended cage through a small window was alternately cut off and exposed by the turning blades of the windmill. The picture of the cage which Rembrandt saw was strikingly clear, whole, and self-contained in features and background. Van Loon represents Rembrandt as having considered this incident the dominating experience in his life because it revealed to him how a painter should see and organize each motif he paints.

Whether Rembrandt actually had such an experience or not was unimportant, but the principle used by Van Loon to explain how Rembrandt might have got his great concern for organic unity in his paintings seemed most apt. It is common knowledge that objects suddenly exposed to light against a background of darkness form unusually vivid images. Such images appear as wholes and are much more vividly recalled than images of objects seen in constant light. For example, note the clearness with which one sees objects suddenly illuminated by flashes of lightning on a pitch black night. If a studio could be equipped to expose models by flashes of light, therein might be a means of teaching students to see with perceptual unity.

Equipping a studio for such work was the next problem. It fortunately was solved by a chance visit to a psychological laboratory in which we saw lantern slides exposed briefly by means of a tachistoscopic attachment, a device for controlling the time a slide is projected on the screen. With such a device, models could be presented through the slides, and the length of exposure of each model could be easily controlled. This seemed to be just the equipment needed.

The problems did not end here, however. What models should be presented on the lantern slides? How long should the exposures be? Should students learn to see and then

---

[1] An extensive collection of reproductions from the Venetians, El Greco, Claude Lorrain, Poussin, Rubens, Goya, Turner, Constable, and Delacroix, as well as from Masaccio, Rembrandt, and Cézanne, were assembled and analyzed in terms of the basic principles of visual form. Common elements appeared in the work of all the masters which could very effectively be understood and explained in terms of perceptual unity. See Appendix C.

[2] For the full text of the story, see Hendrick William Van Loon, *R.v.R.* (Horace Liveright, 1930), pp. 385-389.

to draw, or should drawing be done along with the training in seeing? If one learned to see with perceptual unity in the dark, could he retain the skill when eventually he was required to work in full light? What effect would the two-dimensional character of the screen image have when three-dimensional models were introduced? What else would be needed in the teaching process to ensure that seeing with perceptual unity could be efficiently converted into drawing with compositional unity? These and many other problems remained to be thought through. Solutions suggested themselves in rapid succession, however, as one idea led to another around the common theme of unity — unity in seeing, unity in the process of seeing-and-drawing, unity in the total creative act.

In the fall of 1942, means were obtained to carry through the first experiments. Data were carefully collected on two groups of students, and it is these data, primarily, which are reported in Chapter Four. Several other groups have taken the training since. All our classes in beginning drawing since the fall of 1943 have been taught by these methods. Experience has thus been gained in the use of the methods with over 250 students. Refinements in equipment and technique are continually being made, but the basic principles and procedures have changed little since the first experimental groups were trained. Each day and week bring fresh evidence and a deepened conviction in ourselves and other observers that the methods succeed and that the underlying concept is fundamental.

Chapter Two

PRINCIPLES CONTROLLING THE TEACHING PROGRAM

Introduction and Summary of Principles

THUS FAR, the point has been made that the art of getting compositional unity in a drawing is initially dependent upon the artist's ability to see a motif with perceptual unity. This, however, is but the beginning phase of the seeing-and-drawing process. Between the act of seeing the motif with unity and completing the drawing with unity, there are many elements which may intrude to destroy the effectiveness of the final drawing. The full process, from beginning to end, must have unity: the motif must be seen with perceptual unity; the artist in himself must be free to react as a unit physically, psychologically, and intellectually; the environment in which the artist works must be one with him in supporting and fulfilling his unified reaction; and his techniques of drawing must be free instruments for the unified expression of all these elements in the completed work.

The critical problem in teaching drawing to beginners is that of getting conditions which foster, and in so far as possible require, an organic type of integration among all these elements as the student moves through the complete seeing-and-drawing act. This is the focus of the entire teaching program.

Let us consider the conditions which need to be provided at many different points in the teaching program to get the continuous flow of desired unified reaction. We shall discuss fourteen essential conditions, each with a statement of a general principle and a note on how practical provisions are made in the teaching program to secure the effects desired.

The major principles, in summary, are:

1. The eyes must be trained to see with perceptual unity.

2. Drawing must be accepted as an artificial form, and students must be taught to convert the multi-dimensional quality of things in nature into the two-dimensional terms of the paper.

3. Students must develop a sense for positional relationships and learn to experience other qualities of space and form in terms of positional relationships.

4. Students must develop an ability to see familiar objects in terms of visual qualities, and they must develop this ability to the degree that prior associations with such objects will have only a secondary or a submerged role during the drawing act.

5. Seeing must be developed as an aggressive act.

6. An image seen with perceptual unity must be drawn without the interference of any competing image which might arise externally or in the mind of the student.

7. The attitude of the students during their work must be such as to allow the image seen with perceptual unity to be the organizing agent in the reaction.

8. As seeing moves into drawing during the seeing-and-drawing act, the students must have a clear opportunity to convert visual relations and reactions into kinesthetic and tactile relations and reactions.

9. The whole body must be free to participate in the kinesthetic reactions.

10. The thrill of the experience for the students must flow primarily from the process of seeing-and-drawing; the drawings, as end-products, must be taken as instrumental to experiencing the process.

11. The way must be open for each individual student to express his unique reactions.

12. Seeing-and-drawing must be taught through experience in seeing-and-drawing; there are no substitutes.

13. The guiding discipline must come from the requirements of the process of seeing-and-drawing, and not from the personal authority of the teacher.

14. The program of teaching must have unity from beginning to end; experiences offered in the program must have an orderly progression, with careful timing, so that each act or phase helps to develop and unfold each subsequent act or phase.

How each principle leads to certain practical applications in the design and operation of the teaching program is discussed below:

1. *The eyes must be trained to see with perceptual unity.*

It is a psychological fact that, if a person looks attentively at an object without moving his eyes, he will see it as a perceptual unit. If one is exposed to an object for so short a time that his eyes cannot move, he is automatically required to see it with perceptual unity. The time span for such a flash is one-tenth of a second or less.

Beginning students who both *see and draw* from models flashed for one-tenth of a

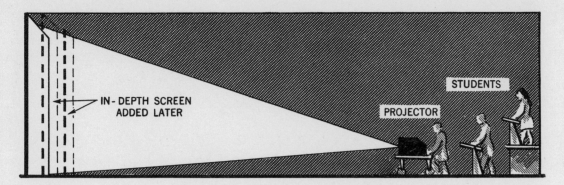

Figure 1. Cross section of laboratory.

second get experience in the full reaction of seeing-and-drawing with perceptual unity. If the teacher gradually increases the time span and the complexity of the drawing problem and keeps his students at this training until their response becomes habitual, he can lead the students to the point where they are able to work from the usual models under ordinary lighting conditions without losing their skill in perceptual unity. A tachistoscope or a shutter on a lantern-slide projector or an ordinary flood lamp turned quickly on and off by hand is a simple and effective way of flashing models for beginning work.

The darkness required by the flash procedure offers many advantages. The eyes when adapted to darkness[1] are many times more sensitive and are in greater readiness for new visual experiences. The tactile sense is stimulated so that the "feel" of the plane on which the drawing is done is more acute. The students cannot see what they are drawing and are forced to use their hands as the chief means of control, thereby coming more quickly to a necessary faith in muscular movements as major controls in the drawing act. All irrelevant subject matter is hidden, leaving the models as the only objects to be exposed by the flashes of light. The drawing problem is clearly presented, free of the usual distractions, and easily controlled.

2. *Drawing must be accepted as an artificial form, and students must be taught to convert the multi-dimensional quality of things in nature into the two-dimensional terms of the paper.*

Since a drawing is done on a two-dimensional surface, it is a highly artificial form, controlled by the rigid limitations of two-dimensional space. Seeing with perceptual unity must, then, become a skill not only in seeing all points in relation to a focal point, but also in converting multi-dimensional relations among these points into two-dimensional terms.

In the beginning, it is easiest for students to see and draw from models which are not multi-dimensional. They are therefore started on lantern-slide images which are, of course, two-dimensional. Later, two or more screens are used in different planes to catch

---

[1] After ten minutes in the dark, the retina of the eye becomes 800 times more sensitive to light.

parts of the same lantern-slide projection, thus introducing a problem part way along the road to multi-dimensional models. (See Figure 1.) Then simple three-dimensional models suspended in air and flashed by a flood lamp to get a temporary effect of two-dimensionality are used. (See Figure 4.) Eventually the students are able to see and control in two-dimensional terms the multi-dimensional forms presented in the normal landscape or studio-model problem.

3. *Students must develop a sense for positional relationships and learn to experience other qualities of space and form in terms of positional relationships.*

The position, size, and brightness of objects affect the way objects are perceived in space. Among these three qualities, position is the most fundamental, since seeing many points with relation to a focal point means sensing the position of the points in relation to each other. Sensitivity to position is, therefore, a critical ability for which ample training should be provided early in the program. A sensitivity to position having been acquired, variations in terms of size and brightness can enter and be interpreted as functions of position.

In developing sensitivity to position, advantage can be taken of the fact that, among the several shapes which might be offered for treatment, the elongated shape is kinesthetically the easiest to draw and optically the easiest to appreciate for its positional quality.[2] Also significant is the fact that masses placed near the edges of a field of vision make more demands upon a sense of position than do masses near the center of the field. The first models to be used, therefore, emphasize elongated masses near the edges of the field. Lantern-slide images are easy to create for this purpose. Use of slides also allows for the gradual inclusion of shapes of various sizes and values as the instructor needs them in building a progression through position, size, and brightness. (See Figure 2.)

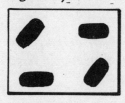      

Position   Size   Brightness

Figure 2.

___

2 Of interest at this point is a story told of Delacroix: " 'Look here for a moment,' and he (Delacroix) draws some ovals on a piece of paper, which he *connects* by fine lines, which are almost *invisible,* and develops a prancing horse full of life and action. 'That,' he says, 'is what Gericault and Gros learned from the *Greeks.*' They expressed first the mass (nearly always oval-shaped) and then the contour. The action should be deduced from the position and proportion of those ovals, and Delacroix says that this was pointed out to him first by Gericault.
"Don't you think that this is a splendid truth?
"Do you learn that from the *draughtsmen of plaster casts* and in the Academy? I think not. If they gave instruction like that, then I would be enthusiastic about the Academy, but I know only too well that such is not the case."
Vincent Van Gogh, *Letters to an Artist* (New York: The Viking Press, 1936), pp. 194-195.

4. *Students must develop an ability to see familiar objects in terms of visual qualities, and they must develop this ability to the degree that old associations with such objects will have only a secondary or a submerged role during the seeing-and-drawing act.*

Teaching people to see with perceptual unity is as much an unlearning process as it is a learning one. Most objects in our adult environment have become familiar through many associations. Rather than being seen for themselves, these objects serve merely as symbols for still other things with which our minds become occupied. We are no longer attentive to the optical forms of things in their optical background. Training students so that they can become attentive to visual qualities and relationships is a matter of breaking these crusts of conventional reaction and introducing a fresh approach to the seeing act.

For effecting this break, the students are plunged immediately into a situation which sharply contrasts with any comparable situation they have known in the past. The darkness of the studio, the flashing of lantern-slides, the stimulation to kinesthetic rather than verbal reactions, the playing of music, the rapid tempo of activity — these and other unusual conditions in the classroom stimulate the students to be fully alive, aware, and, attentive to things going on.

Figure 3.

In addition, the students start drawing from models which are abstract in quality and free of prior associations. On the lantern slides the forms used are simple shapes which are significant only in terms of the seeing-and-drawing acts they require — elongated masses, large and small spots, narrow and wide lines, curves, etc., which create problems in visual form but not in·associated psychological content. (See Figure 3.) Later in the experience, when lantern slides are no longer needed and more familiar objects are introduced, these objects (such as a chair, a wastepaper basket, etc.) are suspended from the ceiling on cords so that they appear unassociated with familiar settings. (See Figure 4.) By the end of the training period, habits in seeing the visual qualities of models are well enough established in most students to permit them to work on landscapes and nudes without old associations rising up to kill the seeing act.

5. *Seeing must be developed as an aggressive act.*

If a student is passive and inattentive when looking at a motif, he will not see it with perceptual unity. There needs to be as much of "reaching out and seizing" the image as of "receiving" it. In the beginning, students need practice in establishing this aggressive frame of mind.

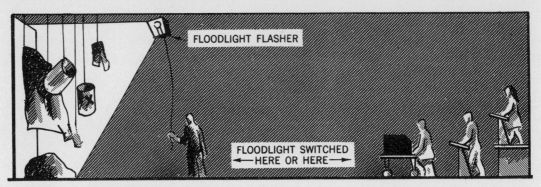

FLOODLIGHT FLASHER

FLOODLIGHT SWITCHED
← HERE OR HERE →

Figure 4.

Conditions for such practice are provided by the surprise element in suddenly flash-ing the model and by accelerating the pace for the full seeing - and - drawing act. Each problem is made very short and several problems are run in quick succession. A warning is given, the model is flashed, the drawing is done in a matter of seconds, the paper is turned over in readiness for the next problem, a warning is given, etc.—all in rhythmic sequence through twenty problems which are completed in about twenty-five minutes.

As the attitude of active response becomes habitual, longer problems are introduced until typical ones can be handled under normal conditions without loss of dynamic quality.[3]

6. *An image seen with perceptual unity must be drawn without the interference of any competing image which might arise externally or in the mind of the student.*

A student is permitted to see a model for less than one-tenth of a second so that there will be but one image seen, and no more. After the model is flashed, no further objects should be seen until the drawing is completed. Particularly, the student should not see his own drawing while it is in process, for in doing so, he tends to form notions of how it might be made to look. These new projections then compete with the original image seen with perceptual unity.

The room in which the drawing is done is therefore made completely dark at first, so that no objects, lights, or other visual distractions are seen. After some weeks the light can be left on, and students may be allowed to look at their drawings as much as they like. Generally, however, students trained in this fashion will need to look at their drawings-in-process relatively little, since, even in complex problems, their controls over the drawings are primarily kinesthetic rather than optical.

7. *The attitude of the students during their work must be such as to allow the image seen with perceptual unity to be the organizing agent in the reaction.*

---

[3] On the point of active response, Delacroix said, "If you are not accomplished enough to make a sketch of a man in mid-air, falling out of a window, in the time it takes him to travel from the fourth floor to the ground, you will never be able to do great work."

Charles de Tolnay, *History and Technique of Old Master Drawings.* (New York: H. Bitner & Company, 1943), p. 12.

As a matter of emphasis, one does not try to *draw* with unity; rather one tries to *see* with unity and to let the image thus seen become the dominating force in organizing the drawing. If the student consciously works at getting unity in his drawing, the effect will be stilted. If, however, he concentrates on the image and relaxes on the mechanics, the drawing will tend to take on the unity desired. The discipline of creative work in the visual arts, in other words, consists more in ruling out extraneous stimulations to muscular action than in aggressively forcing the charcoal or paintbrush here and there on the paper. The body "knows how" to draw, so to speak, if it is but permitted to draw in accordance with the full dictates of the creating image. This means taking the emphasis off the manual manipulations so that the act of drawing can be instrumental rather than primary.

In the teaching program, the techniques of drawing are given only the most incidental attention. Less than a minute is used to suggest to the students how to hold and manipulate charcoal. When work with paints is begun, less than ten minutes are taken to explain mixing paints, building up colors, holding the brush, and other technical points. No one is told how to make lines, values, and hues to get a "proper" effect. These matters are all treated as incidental, great care being taken not to fix the student's attention on them.

8. *As seeing moves into drawing during the seeing-and-drawing act, the students must have a clear opportunity to convert visual relations and reactions into kinesthetic and tactile relations and reactions.*

Though sensitivity to optical relations is primary in the initiation of the seeing-and-drawing act, sensitivity to kinesthetic and tactile relations is primary in the process of forming the drawing. A model visually perceived becomes a form to be kinesthetically and tactually organized. Proportions, distances, positions, and shapes originating as visual measurements have to be interpreted and controlled as kinesthetic and tactile measurements.

To secure this transition from one medium of control to another, the situation is arranged in the beginning of the teaching program so that there is a clear operational difference between the acts of seeing and drawing. Students are given the flash to see by, and then in complete darkness are required to depend on their kinesthetic and tactile senses to guide the making of the drawing. In this way the full energy of the students is focused first in the channel of seeing, then is transferred in clear-cut fashion into kinesthetic and tactile channels for effecting the drawing. The heightened intensity of effort in each phase increases the speed of learning.

Integration is provided between the two phases by the rapid tempo of the total seeing-and-drawing act. The image seen with perceptual unity is maintained throughout as the organizing agent. Before the teaching program ends, the artificial split in the timing of the two phases can be abandoned.

9. *The whole body must be free to participate in the kinesthetic reactions.*

The best drawing is a kinesthetic expression of the whole body. The fingers, hands, and arms alone do not do all the work. The feet, the legs, the muscles of the abdomen— all the motor elements in the body participate. It is important that the body have full freedom to take part in the drawing act.

To help promote this freedom, students stand while they draw. Music is provided by a phonograph on which are played records, usually modern dance tunes, of the students' own choosing. The function of the music is not to set the "mood" or stimulate the "fancy" of the students, but to keep the body attuned to its full possibility of movement and to "draw off" the excess of attention which the students might otherwise give to the particular muscular movements which the manipulation of the charcoal may seem to require.

The room selected for the work is large, without fixed furniture, and without any obstructions or delicate surfaces which might suggest restriction of movement. Images on the screen are nine feet by twelve feet, unusually large for models in a closed room. All the early drawing is done with charcoal or lecturer's crayon on newsprint, eighteen inches by twenty-four inches. Movements required are gross, demanding large muscle participation. No attention is given to detail or exactness.

In the beginning, courage to make bold and expressive masses is needed in order to enable students to develop the feeling of kinesthetic participation of their bodies as a whole. As the training progresses, the models are made more complex to increase the demand for more exact placement. Ultimately the students are introduced to problems which require clear definition of quite small shapes in an intricate background. However, this kind of work is not undertaken until participation by the body is learned as habit.

10. *The thrill of the experience for the students must flow primarily from the process of seeing-and-drawing; the drawings, as end-products, must be taken as instrumental to experiencing the process.*

The results of drawing are not to be measured primarily in terms of the end-product. If students or instructor get the notion that the pictures created are the be-all and end-all of the enterprise, students will fail to learn drawing as an experience and for that reason will also fail to produce a drawing of much significance for other people.

One does not achieve a drawing of deep significance for other people by deliberately setting out to produce such a drawing. Rather, one first learns how to be true to his own expression possibilities and requirements. If it happens that his possibilities and requirements are of a character to harmonize with the possibilities and requirements of other people, then one will achieve something which other people will value. But this is an incidental result and cannot be taken as a primary aim.

12

To take the emphasis off the end-product, the instructor abstains from criticising or publicly judging a student's drawing as an end-product. He takes each drawing into account in relation to the individual producing it and to the circumstances under which it is produced. He seldom speaks to a student about a drawing, and the students themselves are given little opportunity to ponder over the work they have completed.

The important value is the intrinsic quality of the whole active experience for the individual student at the time the drawing is being made: the awareness of self it creates, the freedom of expression it releases, the kinesthetic satisfactions it allows, the intellectual relaxation it provides, the creative fun of it. These aspects of the experience are, of course, not the conscious aims of the drawing act at the time the drawing is made, but are the means by which the value of the experience is built up in the student and judged by the instructor. The student's conscious aim, as pointed out earlier, is to see the image and to let the image take form on paper.

Near the end of the training period, habits are well enough formed to permit the instructor to suggest methods and techniques in the handling of media used when and if the student, in pursuit of his expression, seems able to benefit from and appreciate such suggestions. Not until then does the instructor intrude his suggestions upon the student, and even then, all such suggestions are kept in the framework of helping the student to fulfill his own possibilities and requirements.

11. *The way must be open for each individual student to express his own reactions.*

Each individual has his own unique approach to each drawing problem. Students, drawing from the same model, will produce different drawings and will ascribe different meanings to the experience they have had. These differences arise from the unique interests, experiences, sensitivities, and skills of each personality. Such differences are necessary and desirable; uniformity in results is neither desirable nor possible.

For a student to *try* to be different, however, is for him to make as much of a mistake as he would make if he tried to get a product which met some standard of uniformity. The student's individuality should appear in his drawing as an incidental aspect of his work rather than as a conscious aim.

The instructor, therefore, takes care to avoid both an emphasis on individuality as such and on uniformity as such. He abstains from any comments to individuals which would cause them artificially to prize their individuality. He also abstains from any pronouncements of his own standards for any given drawing. Students leave at the end of the course without knowing what kind of finished product the instructor happens, in his own personal taste, to like best. All procedures are avoided which would cause students to pit themselves against each other in competition for any set goal. When grades are necessary, they are given on the basis of individual considerations, emphasizing attitudes and motivation rather than quality of the end-product.

12. *Seeing-and-drawing must be taught through experience in seeing-and-drawing; there are no substitutes.*

Learning is most efficient when the basic controls over the student flow from the seeing-and-drawing process. The process sets the challenge and teaches the procedure. Consequently, the program is filled with the activity of seeing-and-drawing and with little else.

Particularly, there is no talk about art. Such talk usually does more harm than good with beginning students. It causes them to develop verbal avenues of association which stir them toward intellectualizations and self-centeredness at the very moment when they should be freely optical, kinesthetic, and expressive in their reactions. Hence there is no talk about drawing, about great artists, about the history of art, or about any other subjects which tend to establish verbalisms instead of drawing reactions. The only talk in the laboratory is about things having little or no relation to art—baseball games, the music, chit-chat, banter. Even at the end of the training period, the students do not know the technical words for many of the simplest aspects of the work. When they become fully independent and stable in their power to see-and-draw with unity, verbal treatments of the usual subjects of art may be undertaken without danger, and indeed, with far more power for imparting full meanings.

13. *The guiding discipline must come from the requirements of the process of seeing-and-drawing, and not from the personal authority of the teacher.*

The role of the instructor in teaching drawing is to set up the situation so that the process of seeing-and-drawing, and *not* the instructor, becomes the psychologically dominant element in the classroom. The instructor takes great care not to become identified as the "instructor" or the "authority." His role is quite casual and is seemingly incidental to the main features of the situation. Psychologically, his chief function in the class is to spread a contagion of informality and freedom and to give the students encouragement and confidence that what they are doing in this strange, new experience is good. The students come to look on the instructor as a companion with them in their own new and, at first, queer adventures.

There is one situation in which the instructor intrudes upon a student. If a student, after having learned to see and to draw with perceptual unity, drops back into his old habits, the instructor will call that fact to the student's attention. The habit of seeing with perceptual unity, once learned, must not be broken. In such instances, the instructor expects, if necessary, to arouse a certain amount of emotional reaction (surprise, amusement, sometimes anger), since deep-seated habits are not to be broken by rational appeals alone. In these cases, however, the instructor takes care to let the students see that he is acting out of respect for the demands of the process rather than out of any desire to get the students to do what he wants done, simply because he is the instructor. Students catch the difference, and realize that they are being challenged by the discipline of the process, not by the discipline of a personal authority.

14. *The program of teaching must have unity from beginning to end; experiences offered in the program must have an orderly progression, with careful timing, so that each act or phase helps to develop and unfold each subsequent act or phase.*

To a very important degree, the success of the training program depends upon the proper ordering of the various elements at play in the process. The progression needs to be such that as one habit is achieved, it may be exercised and depended upon while other habits are being built. The pace of the sequence should be such as to bring changes as soon as the students are able to take them; there should be no dallying at any given level in the progression. All the basic elements required in the full flowering of the seeing-and-drawing act should be present in the "bud" at the beginning. Each element should be sufficiently isolated to be defined, recognized, and manipulated, but one element should never be introduced as something to be worked on apart from the other elements with which it operates in the total process; each part is much more easily mastered when it is a function of a whole.

At the beginning of the program, many temporary aids are needed to focus reaction in terms of a few of the most basic learnings required. As the program progresses, these aids are dropped one by one until, at the end, they are not needed at all. As a strong emphasis is placed upon one phase of the development, it is often necessary to reintroduce aids previously dropped in other phases in order to allow the students full energy for the newly dominating demand. The various elements must be so interwoven as to support each other in the growth of the total process.

These are some of the chief points to which the instructor is sensitive in guiding the sequence of activities in the teaching program. The pattern of development is not unlike that of a symphony wherein the opening notes give the theme and succeeding notes introduce the variations, with sometimes this part of the theme dominant and sometimes that, until the music gets its full power. The handling of the progression is an artistic act, depending on the instructor's creative sense to determine what the experience next allows and requires.

The following outline shows some of the elements taken into account and the status of each element at the beginning and before the end of the training period. The order in which the elements are listed has no special significance.

Element	At The Beginning	Before The End
Location of the work	In the studio	Outdoors, wherever necessary
Lighting of the studio	Complete darkness	Full normal light
Media used	Charcoal, lecturer's crayon	Paints, four colors
Forms used as models	Lantern slides	Landscapes, nudes
Nature of the shapes	Simple, elongated shapes	Varied, full range
Size of the shapes	Roughly uniform	Varied, full range
Number of shapes	Three or four	Unlimited
Pattern of shapes	Simple, large, plain	Complex, varied, subtle
Exposure of light on forms	One-tenth of a second	Sustained

Element	At the Beginning	Before the End
Range of tones	Black on white	Varied, full range
Range of color	Black or white	Varied, full range
No. of dimensions in form	Two-dimensional	Multi-dimensional
Distance from forms	Far away (55 ft.)	Close (10 ft.) or as far as needed
Angle of vision	Normal	Unusually wide, demanding
Center of focus	Constant: center of screen	Free and self-selected
Kinesthetic stimulation	Music continuously	Music not used
Talk about art	Never done	Done with individual cases

Summary Focused on Teaching Methods

Before turning to the next chapter, which will show more clearly how the program progresses in its concrete phases, it may be helpful to summarize the foregoing fourteen points from a different angle. The emphasis in these points has been upon the principles which explain the "why" of the unusual procedures characterizing much of the teaching program. To summarize now in terms of the procedures indicated, the principles establish the case that beginning students will be most efficient in learning to draw and paint if, in the beginning of the training program:

they learn to draw in the dark;

they see each model but once, see it in a flash, and see nothing else until they finish drawing it;

they draw from models which are big, two-dimensional, abstract patterns simply but carefully designed;

they learn positional relationships first, and size, brightness, color, etc. later as functions of position;

they work rapidly and rhythmically—see first and draw second to complete each time the full cycle of the seeing-and-drawing act;

they work with big movements, large muscle participation, and full freedom for bodily action;

they are active and alert in their seeing, relaxed in their drawing;

they never work on techniques as techniques;

they work for the fun of the process, not for the "perfect" drawing;

they express themselves as individuals;

they do not intellectualize or verbally analyze—do not hear talk about how they should draw or about how others do draw.

Experience has proved that teaching guided by these principles of method can be productive of unusual results. The next chapter shows, in narrative and descriptive manner, how the classroom program unfolds. We shall then describe results obtained with experimental groups.

Chapter Three

DESCRIPTION OF THE
TEACHING PROGRAM

Setting and Equipment

THE STUDIO used during the training periods is a large room, sixty feet long, forty feet wide, and fifteen feet high. The walls, floors, and ceiling are monotones, low in value, with little color, and unbroken by any sharp lines or masses. The whole gives a feeling of spaciousness. The drawing tables at which the students stand to work are arranged in the rear of the room. The large screen, twenty-two feet long and fifteen feet high, on which the lantern-slide images are projected, hangs in the front of the room. Two flanking, movable screens which may be used for special effects are also available. (See Figures 5 and 6.) The lantern-slide projector and record player are placed about three-fourths of the way from the front of the room. A flood lamp, used when three-dimensional models are employed, is placed to the left. All furniture in the room is movable and frequently is moved in the course of the program.

Students come to the class for one period a day, five days a week, for six weeks. The class period usually lasts no more than thirty-five minutes until late in the project when more demanding problems require longer time. Each student is given twenty sheets of newsprint and large sticks of charcoal or crayon. When work with paints is begun, the students use No. 6 brushes and a special quick-drying protein paint. The painting is done on No. 5 chip board, a weight which is sufficiently thick to prevent warping and yet is economical.

Procedure with Lantern Slides

Lantern-slide projections are the models from which the students first draw. This phase of the work usually takes about four weeks or twenty periods. The routine is roughly the same each day. When the student enters the room, he goes to his place and arranges his board and equipment in position to work. The lights are turned off, and the students sit in the darkness for about ten minutes while their eyes are becoming adapted to the darkness. During the interval music is played, and the students sing, whistle, or beat time. The dominant activity during this period is the tapping of feet. Occasionally a comment is made about the day's work.

Figure. 5. Arrangement of main screens and spot lines.

Figure 6. Arrangement of flanking screens.

When the eyes are "dark-adapted," the students take their places for work. The instructions given the first few times are about as follows:

> Continue to respond to the music. Keep relaxed. Run your fingers over the surface and around the edges of the paper to sense its location and size. After you have finished a drawing, turn the sheet over quickly. Try to keep the whole period of drawing in rhythmic sequence; draw with big movements, feel the movements throughout your whole body; draw vigorously and with conviction. Ready!

A warning is given shortly before each slide is flashed. Twenty slides are exposed and drawn during a period. The time taken for this work is about twenty minutes. Beginning in the third week, about five minutes at the close of each period is spent in quickly repeating the slides while the student looks at the drawing he has made from each slide.

The slides are designed with considerable care. About four hundred slides are necessary for the complete project. The shapes are drawn to provide an increasing complexity in position, size, configuration, and value. The early slides are simple problems in position, in which elongated masses are roughly sketched. About three or four such masses are drawn on a slide, graduating into more precise shapes, differing in character, tonal quality, and dimensions. (See Figures 7, 8, 9, and 10.)

At approximately the twelfth drawing period, an old-master color reproduction is placed before the students. They are instructed to continue the pattern of reaction used for the slide drawings. This practice is continued for several periods as the last phase of each day's work. For this work, the light is kept on continuously. The chief purpose in this variation is to assure the students that they are really learning to draw.

During the four weeks when lantern slides are used, the students are progressively brought closer to the screen. They begin at about fifty-five feet from the screen, and by the end of the four weeks are working at fifteen feet. The required angle of vision shifts from a comfortable 10° at the beginning to a demanding 35° at the end. This shift of position increases by twelve times the field of vision to be kept under control. The purpose of this shift is to increase the student's capacity to see and draw a broad field.

Changes are also made in the screen on which the images are projected. Work starts with the usual single screen. About the third week, however, two additional screens are used. (See Figure 6.) These are placed about five feet in front of the original screen in such a position as to catch part of the projected image on each side, while the center of the image is still on the original screen. This procedure introduces a transition from the two-dimensional projections to the three-dimensional models. As a further step, the students are asked to draw from images projected on the floor[1] and on the ceiling. (See Figures 11 and 12.) When they are able to solve these problems well, the students are ready to draw from three-dimensional models.

---

[1] This has later proven to be of great value in solving the "foreground" problem of landscape.

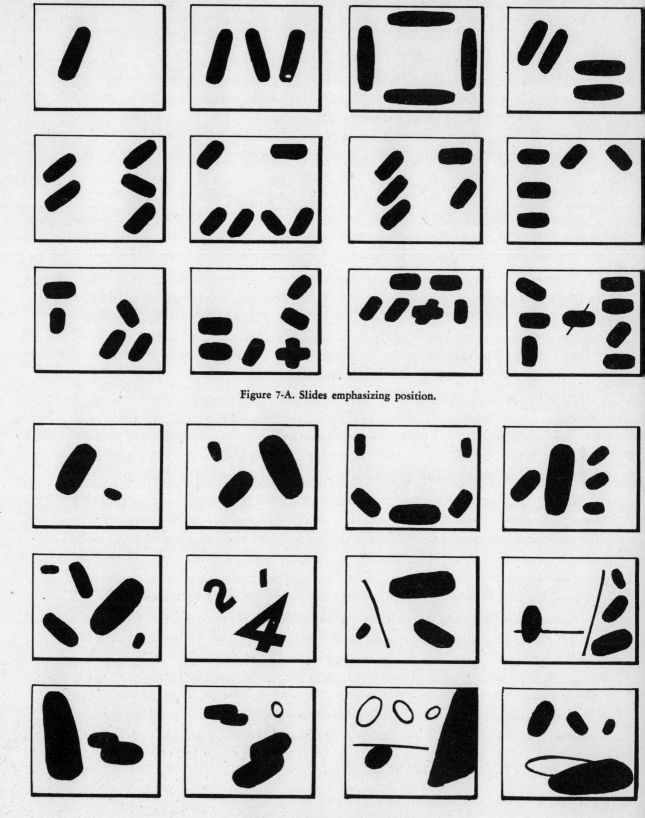

Figure 7-A. Slides emphasizing position.

Figure 7-B. Slides emphasizing size.

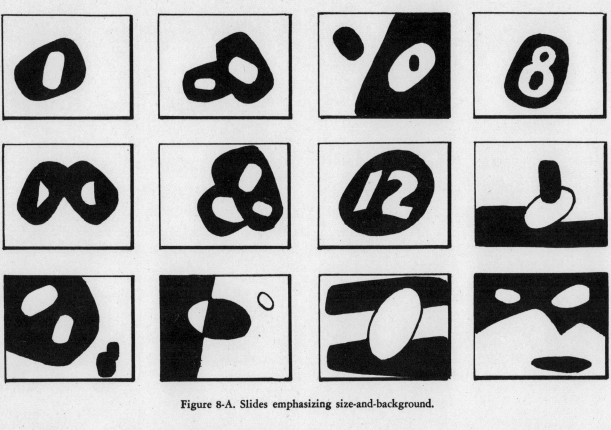

Figure 8-A. Slides emphasizing size-and-background.

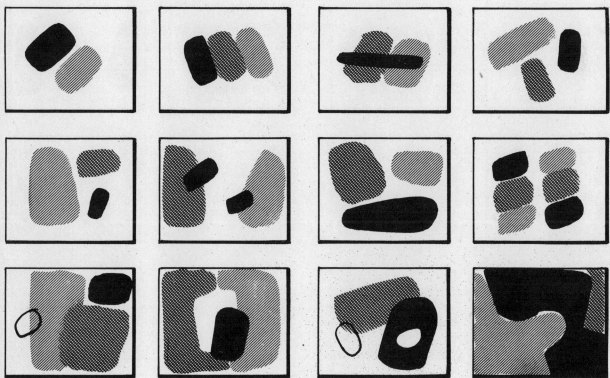

Figure 8-B. Slides emphasizing brightness.

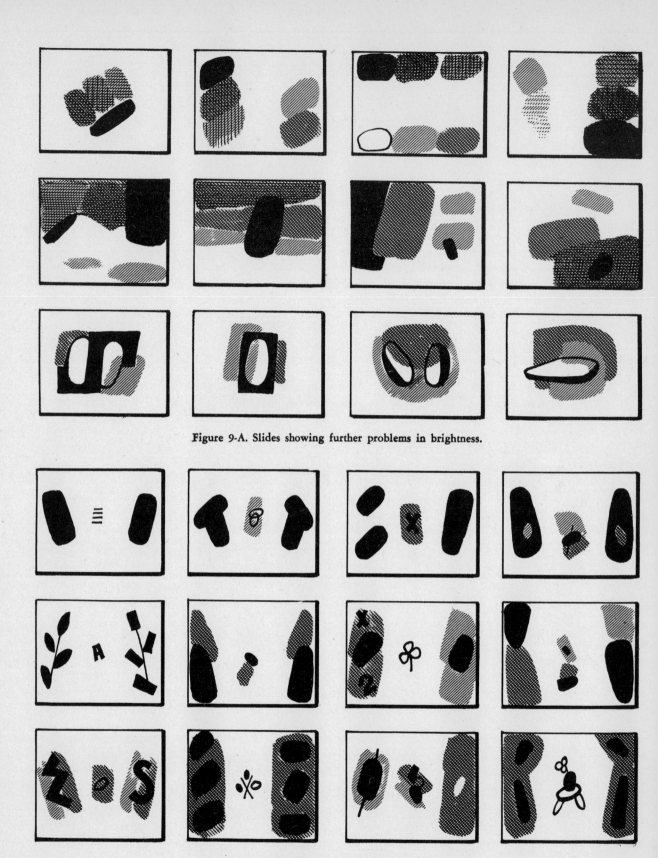

Figure 9-A. Slides showing further problems in brightness.

Figure 9-B. Slides used with flanking screens.

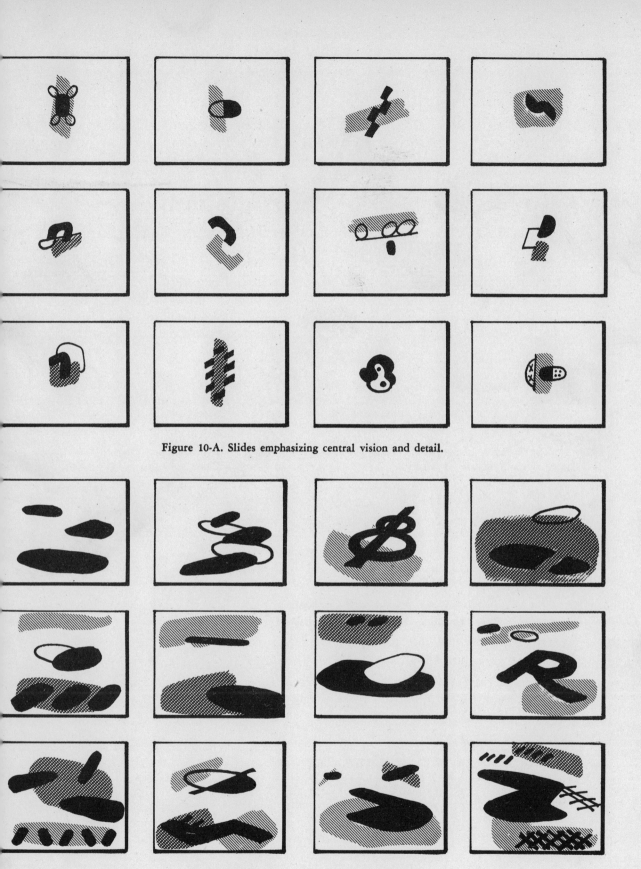

Figure 10-A. Slides emphasizing central vision and detail.

Figure 10-B. Slides used in floor projection.

Figure 11.

To facilitate training in tonal values, gray and eventually black curtains are suspended over part or all of the screen. This makes it more difficult to distinguish slight variations in value and challenges the students to a finer perception. Students are also forced to realize that the background in a drawing is as dynamic in its power of forming an image as is the main feature. Thus they learn that all parts of the drawing surface must be rendered with equal effectiveness and must be given equal care.

Procedure with Three-Dimensional Models

The transition to work with three-dimensional forms is begun in the fourth week, along with work on the slides. By the fifth week, three-dimensional models are used almost entirely. The first models are suspended from the ceiling by small cords so that they stand out in space and have no clear association with any customary setting. Familiar objects, such as a chair, or wastebasket, or a gasoline can, when suspended in space have the effect of abstract forms. For illumination, a flood lamp is flashed on and off as quickly as possible. (See Figure 13.) The students stand in the rear of the room. A small flashlight is used to project a red spot upon the ensemble. By changing the position of the spot and by moving the students from point to point in the room, we provide experience with a changed center of focus. The same ensemble, viewed from different angles, with different centers of focus, makes different pictures. Toward the end of this phase of the work, the floodlight is left on for longer periods of time. Finally, normal light is used, and the students may look at their papers while drawing.

Toward the end of the fifth week, a dancer is used as a model during one period. She dances in the darkness. A floodlight is flashed and in the darkness the students draw from the pose they have seen. Several such drawings are made in

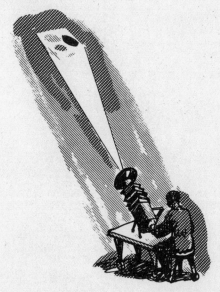

Figure 12.

24

quick succession. The last period before shifting from charcoal to paint is spent out-of-doors drawing landscapes.

Procedure with Paint

During the sixth and last week of the training period, the students use paints. A special protein paint (soy bean) is used because of its quick-drying quality, brilliance, great covering power, and plasticity. In the beginning, the paint is premixed in three values—black, dark gray, and white. The floodlight is kept on. Models first used are the familiar objects previously drawn with charcoal. Soon, however, ensembles containing detail are set up in a corner of the room and are drawn from a near-by position.

After the monochrome phase of painting, the students are given one color, such as green, red, or brown, in addition to the black and white. An ensemble is set up in which the chosen color is present, so arranged as to require the use of the black and white to effect the proper values. One painting in this medium is completed, and the students are ready for work outside the laboratory, using a range of four colors. After a few moments of spotting the broad generalizations, the students proceed to paint a landscape. Usually not more than two landscape problems are required.

As a final problem, the students are brought back into the laboratory to do a charcoal drawing of a nude model. A few flash exposures are made for rapid preliminary sketches; and then the students do the complete problem.

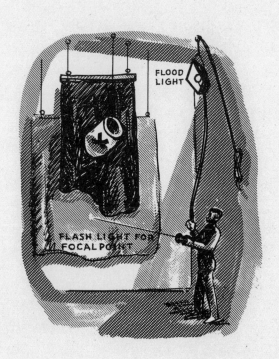

FLOOD LIGHT

FLASH LIGHT FOR FOCAL POINT

Figure 13.

Chapter Four

RESULTS OF THE
TEACHING PROGRAM

Source and Nature of the Data

APPROXIMATELY 250 students have thus far completed the seeing-and-drawing program. The general experience of the writer and other teachers with the total group contributes materially to the discussion in this chapter. The detailed data on which the discussion focuses, however, come from the first two classes to take the work. Research facilities were available in the first two classes which have not been available since. This means that while the number of cases on which the discussion is directly based is limited, the range of analytical work in interpreting the data and deriving the findings is relatively broad. There are no conclusions with relation to the first two classes which are not supported by general experience with subsequent groups.

All students in the first two classes were volunteers. The first group of twelve, nine men and three women, volunteered from a beginning drawing course. A few of these students expected to become fine arts majors, but the majority were taking beginning drawing as an incidental interest. None had had more than the usual training offered in secondary schools. The second group of thirteen, all men, were volunteers taken at random from freshmen in the College of Education. None of these men had had any previously expressed interest in the arts. Their dominant reason for volunteering was that of helping in an experiment, not that of learning the art of drawing for its own sake.

The fundamental pattern of training for the two classes was the same, but the first was more experimental since the instructor was working out many of the materials, methods, and research techniques as the study went along. Work with the second group settled into channels closely paralleling the program outlined in the preceding chapter, and research techniques were more smoothly operated. When illustrations are needed, most cases are drawn from the second group since the data are more nearly complete.

Three kinds of evidence will now be discussed in this order: the drawings of the students, the students' reactions to the experience, and the results of special tests set up to determine changes in students' visual abilities. We shall then present a summary interpretation of the findings as they relate to this method of teaching beginning drawing and painting.

Results in the Drawings

Each student completed about five hundred exercises during the six weeks. Only a few drawings can be reproduced here. A selection has been made which, in our judgment, is representative of what may be expected from similar groups taught in the same manner. The aim of the selection has been to pick those drawings which seem best for illustrating the variety and range of results. Each drawing is discussed at some length in order to bring into the open those aspects which reflect the effects of the teaching program. We are primarily interested in seeing how the behavior of a student, as recorded in his drawing, is related to the principles on which the teaching program is based.

Adams' and Brown's sketches of the same subject, reproduced in Figures 14 and 15 respectively, illustrate a number of principles. The model was Pascin's "Girl Seated." (Figure 18.) About four minutes were used to complete the drawings. This is the first time these two students had ever attempted a full picture of any kind. They had had no art training prior to entry into the course, and had but six clock hours of laboratory experience, all of which had been spent in making drawings from lantern slides, rather than from the conventional pictorial material.

These two drawings, while differing to a marked degree, nevertheless present the essential character of Pascin's painting. There is no difficulty in sensing this common aspect in the sketches. The marked difference between them reflects the dissimilar ways in which the two students responded to the stimulation of the subject, each in harmony with his own personality. As was pointed out earlier, those who achieve skill in seeing-and-drawing with perceptual unity reflect the level at which their personalities allow them to see.

The most striking quality of Adams' work (Figure 14) is its naiveté. The oversized head is characteristic of drawings made by children and primitives who enlarge that part of a picture which has the most associative value. Adams unconsciously sees at a naive level. Had he been asked to criticize his drawing, he probably would have called it "bad" because it is obviously out of proportion according to commonly accepted standards of which he is intellectually well aware. Had he been trained to present his subject in its intellectually perceived proportions, he would doubtless have experienced a conflict between what his "unconscious" was "wanting" to do and what his mind was telling him he "should do." Consequently, he would have given up in disgust and would have declared that there was nothing in art for him. But the pathways between his seeing and his kinesthetic actions were already well enough formed to permit him to forget the technical problems of drawing, and to work with an ease which permitted his personality to play into the center of the process and place its stamp upon the product. He was released to see the thing as a whole and let his personality as a whole come into the

Figure 14. By Adams.   From Pascin's "Girl Seated."   Figure 15. By Brown.

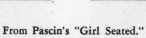

Figure 16. By Carter.   From nude model.   Figure 17. By Duncan.

process. At the same time, he was not an undisciplined and erratic individualist, as is reflected in the fact that his work also contains the stamp of Pascin. A sentimental individualism would have wiped out Pascin altogether. By our definition of what artistic skill should be, Adams, therefore, succeeded.

Brown, in rendering a quite different result — one relatively much more mature in its revealed psychological level — also succeeded. Contradictory as it sounds, his drawing not only has more individuality but also is more representative of Pascin than the work of Adams. The naiveté of Adams is so typical of naiveté generally as to place his drawing in a classical archetype, among all naive works the world over. Brown, on the other hand, has achieved a development which places his

Figure 18. Pascin, "Girl Seated."

work outside any typical group and nearer an individual achievement. He is more than one of the masses; he is well on the way to becoming something in himself — an integrated, individual personality. This appears in his drawing. At the same time, he has abstracted the essence of Pascin with marked success. Had he tried to imitate Pascin, he would never have succeeded; but by crating his own drawing in response to his own personality, he, paradoxically, has also caught the quality of Pascin to an extraordinary degree.[1]

In this dual way, Brown achieved a distinction which makes his work more prized by the current culture than the work of Adams. By current standards, his work is "better," meaning that his personality is more typical of what our culture accepts. But, so far as the drawing teacher was concerned, the behavior of Brown was no "better" than the behavior of Adams. Both students were able freely to express their personalities through their drawing at the level at which their personalities would allow, *and this is one of the prized achievements the teacher is after.* He dare not put the end-product of Brown above that of Adams, or cause end-products to become of primary importance. If it happens that the instructor enjoys one end-product more than another, it must be in the deep privacy of his own soul, and must never interfere with his dominant concern for the

---

[1] In recent decades, we have assumed that this use of the old masters is mere mimicry, and therefore abortive to the development of individuality. In so doing we have failed to understand the paradox whereby individuality and universality issue from the same process. The old masters were themselves trained by the "copying" device, but the secret of their success with the technique was that they re-created rather than imitated the model.

development, in every student, of the skills of unified experiencing and expression which are the artistic process. This is the special discipline of the art teacher's profession.

The sketches by Carter and by Duncan, reproduced in Figures 16 and 17, also offer a contrast in maturity of psychological conception. These drawings were made from a nude model during the final period of the program. About seven minutes were taken for their completion. Neither student had worked from a nude model before.

Nudes sometimes prove difficult to do, not because of visual elements, but because of past associations with the human body. When past associations are sufficiently stimulating and deeply enough entrenched, the newly acquired patterns of seeing-and-drawing with perceptual unity are more likely to be broken and the drawing to be done in relation to old conceptions. The fine organization in Carter's and Duncan's drawings implies that their habits of perceptual unity had become well established.

When habits of perceptual unity are well established, the type of subject matter makes little difference in drawing skill. Whatever the subject, the students are able to handle it with about equal facility. In this experiment, students drew from abstract subjects, reproductions of old masterpieces, still life settings, landscapes, and nudes in rapid succession, without realizing that subject matter itself could offer any special problem.[2] They simply went to work on each model as it appeared. No comments to emphasize differences were made by the instructor. Had differences been emphasized, attention would have been drawn to technical problems, and freedom for the whole experience would have been lost. The success of this procedure suggests that the specialized training on different types of subject matter, such as is usually offered in art teaching, is not desirable with beginning students when they are learning to see and draw with perceptual unity.

This is not to say, however, that differences in subject matter have no effect on the drawings, but rather that, given habits of perceptual unity, the effect is more psychological than optical or kinesthetic. The psychological effect shows in the style with which the subject is treated, but the process of drawing itself varies little in its authority and power from one subject to another. Carter, who showed great naiveté in his treatment of the nude, showed far less naiveté in other subjects and in all his drawings evidenced about the same level of developing skill. The total reaction to the subject was the dominating element, and his technical skill, however varied from the subject to subject, served that reaction. The process of drawing was itself instrumental to the larger experiences.

---

[2] The fact that the students drew from models rather than from "imagination" may raise a question in the minds of some as to the value of this type of training program for those who want to work from images originating from subjective rather than objective sources. The answer is clear when one realizes that the flash procedure is carefully worked out so that the student draws from an image which is within him, after the model is flashed and gone. Whether the image has an objective or subjective source is immaterial. Objective models were used in the training program because they allow for control of the situation while students are learning to use an image as it needs to be used to draw with perceptual unity. Later they can draw from subjective images using the same modes of reaction.

30

Freely flowing technical skill, which releases the personality for participation and expression in the drawing, has many favorable effects. The art products thus created emanate from a level sufficiently deep in human experience to make them worthy of the attention of other people. The nudes of Carter and Duncan, different though they are, are both clear and distilled interpretations which come from "down inside" and which represent something universal enough to catch the attention of the observer and reward him for time spent. Any artistic work which has value for others comes from such levels. With training in perceptual unity, beginning students are tapping these deeper levels.

Even more important than the art product, however, is the fact that expression of personality provides release and stimulation to those who do the drawing. Evidences of such release were constantly appearing in the daily class conduct of the students. The work was recreation. Without knowing why, the students felt something was happening to them which they prized for its personal value. The therapeutic effect of creative expression has long been known and used by psychologists, though most art training has failed to tap these outlets of expression which would bring personality to the fore. Training in perceptual unity, however, opens these outlets.[3]

The instructor viewing many drawings from each student is able to discover a great deal about each personality. To the cues provided by the drawings he is able to add considerable information by carefully observing the students in the free atmosphere of the studio. In the activities of the classroom situation, it was clear, for example, that Carter, whose conception of the human body was naive, as revealed through his drawing, was also naive and undeveloped in his understanding of human relationships. He got along with other students, but he was not sensitive to things which were happening to other people about him. His reactions were typical of a man three or four years younger than he. Duncan, on the other hand, who showed rather unusual maturity and who was entering a profession devoted to the study of people, attracted the respect of other students and had considerable confidence in his own relationships with them. His drawing of the nude was mature.

Such observations the instructor undertakes for the purpose of guiding class activities so that they serve personality in the most meaningful way. Development in drawing and development in personality go hand in hand. The instructor cannot, however, allow himself to get entangled with a student's personal problems, for that would encourage the student to attach himself to the instructor as a personality and would tend to destroy the disciplined relation of the student to his own process of expression. It is im-

---

[3] Clinical psychologists now use creative work for its therapeutic values in treating abnormal cases. The same values may be obtained by the average person if he has the necessary freedom for expression. One of the interests in the development of this method of teaching is to open these avenues to the average person. These students were average students: they were not interested in the arts professionally. The results were gratifying. Further development of training in perceptual unity may open up new notions about the relation between art and personality. It may help to bridge the gap between child and adult art, between primitive and sophisticated art, and between "pure" expressionism and "pure" realism, to name a few of the dichotomies which are unfortunately rampant in our culture.

plicit in the art teacher's profession that his first concern be with the *process,* and that he achieve whatever results he is able to achieve through manipulations in the art sphere, and not in the personal realm.

Duncan's work in Figure 17 reveals a nice sensitivity to problems of texture. Differences between the somewhat flabby flesh of the torso and the more compact flesh of the legs are indicated by nicely varied techniques. Similar competency in handling textural problems is shown in the next drawing, Figure 19, by Brown (who also did Figure 15).

When Brown did the interior represented in Figure 19, he had had about fifteen hours of laboratory work. This was his second experience with the brush. He was given black, white, and gray paints and was started immediately on the project. He finished the painting in about one and one-quarter hours.

The painting appears to us to have all the marks of work done by the so-called "talented" and advanced art student: composition, "deep space," animation in all sections of the painting, and a complex range of values and forms. The draperies "drape"; the walls stand as "walls"; the temporary screens look like "temporary" screens; the window catches and reflects light. Such work suggests that deliberate and self-conscious efforts of students to secure a proper texture is non-essential when the students are able to see and draw with perceptual unity.

Reacting to the "whole," the student also handles the "parts." Simple logic might cause one to assume that an approach in terms of the whole would necessitate a sacrifice in terms of the parts. The relation, however, is not logical but organic. The whole means the functional inclusion of the parts, and the students sense that in order to report their experience of the whole, they need to include the parts in the proper relations. Despite the fact that no instruction was given on how to make the window panes shed light, or how to suggest the difference between a shadow and a substance, Brown gets these differences into his work with marked skill. These textural effects are obtained by following through on the same principles that apply under perceptual unity for handling any problems of space and form, avoiding the error, common when texture is treated as a special problem, of assuming that something new and different, of a special tactile quality, is involved. Under perceptual unity the principles applicable to handling the whole allow for handling the parts.[4]

Brown's first use of color is reproduced as Figure 20. He was given a palette of green, yellow ochre, black, and white. With these limited colors, he succeeded well in the face of the complex range of colors which appeared in nature. He used color as it should be used to fulfill the requirements of space-form. Color is an agent of space re-

---

[4] When a special problem is made of "texture," the temptation is to fall into the error of supposing that the appropriate effect may be obtained by somehow manipulating the brush, paint, and canvas with the same type of kinesthetic response as the object stimulates. Thus students will try to draw hair on the head by making fine flowing strokes resembling individual hairs until the head is built up. Or they will draw a woolly object by getting "woolly" about it. The problem, however, is one of space and form which is subject to the same laws that apply to general problems of space and form. The students in this experiment, already performing in relation to these general laws, went ahead without difficulty, extending their skills to handle problems of texture.

Figure 19. By Brown from room interior.

Figure 20. By Brown from landscape.

lations in the same sense that values are an agent of space relations in the charcoal drawings, except that color offers more complex possibilities for establishing relationships. In its complexity, color demands more of the artist's sensitivity to relationships in the whole field.

However, Brown was not confused by the greater complexity of his medium, and proceeded to use the basic habits he had already developed in black and white to achieve a commendable result in color. He gave reality to the whole canvas and stability to the foreground plane, avoided confusion between local color and broad generalizations, and withstood the temptation to try for "atmospheric" effects—achievements which are often lacking in beginning painters. His placement of detail is confident and right, as witnessed in the sureness with which he placed the two objects in the left foreground (a wastepaper hamper and a fire plug).

Such skills in a first use of color are evidence of the basic nature of the training in perceptual unity. When these paintings were done, all the crutches which had been used in the laboratory were withdrawn; temptations were offered by old associations with nature which normally lead to superficial pictorial effects, and a new, more complex medium was placed in the students' hands. Despite these shocks of change, the transitions were made without loss of skill, attesting, among other things, to the truth of the fundamental assumption that color is best regarded as an extension of the problem of space-form, rather than as something separate to be treated by quite different principles.

Three works by Brown have been reproduced (Figures 15, 19, and 20). In all three, there is a notable tendency toward a linear style and a nice use of value. That such behavior in drawing would be expected from Brown is indicated in the results of the optical tests, subsequently to be discussed in some detail. Brown showed a marked ability in central acuity, central stereo-acuity, and brightness discrimination (see pp. 42 to 47), ranking first or second in the group of students on at least one of the two tests given for each of these three abilities. These particular tests measure sensitivity to line placement and to range of values. These qualities also appear as strong characteristics of the drawing of Brown, attesting to the fact that what the eye is able to do affects what the student is able to do in his drawing.

Evans' drawings (see Figures 21 to 24) present further evidence in the same direction. A glance at his sketches will show that their chief characteristic, as contrasted to those of Brown, is their utilization of masses as a dominant element in the drawings. Evans ranked equally high with Brown on the tests in which Brown ranked high, but in addition, he also ranked at the top of the group on tests given for measuring peripheral acuity and peripheral stereo-acuity. Abilities in peripheral vision indicate a quick and accurate comprehension of masses and broad forms. Having these abilities, Evans capitalized on them as additional and dominant resources for achieving his drawings. With a wider range of top abilities in perception, he had greater flexibility than Brown, and he

Figure 21. Painting from
studio set-up.

Figure 22. Drawing from an old
master reproduction.

Four Pictures by Evans

Figure 23. From nude model.

Figure 24. From landscape.

utilized his extra capacities to advantage. Brown, however, still had a large enough range of abilities to permit him to work with great effectiveness.

Such evidence indicates clearly the intimate and inextricable relation between seeing and drawing. Evidence presented later will show not only that seeing affects drawing, but also that the experience in drawing has an effect upon seeing. Optical abilities are improved by training in drawing.

In the drawings of Evans, and of all those who have facility in drawing with perceptual unity, one will note an artistically satisfying "perspective" and "composition." In much art training, these two qualities are made matters of special attention, students being taught formulas of geometrical perspective and other compositional devices. In the procedures used here, however, these qualities are not given special attention since they are but two of the many dimensions to which the student is sensitive if he sees-and-draws with perceptual unity.

To the students who see with perceptual unity, all the forms in a model appear related to each other. There are no abstracted feelings of near and far, up and down, right and left, as such, but rather the relationships are felt to extend from each form to each other form in the setting. As in the relativity of physics, the dimensions used are functions of the relations of the forms to each other, and are not presumed to extend from the fixed point of the observer. There are as many dimensions to the relations as there are points in the forms related to each other.

For this system of relationships, a dynamic focal point *in the setting* acts as a kind of "clearing house" through which all the relations take order. This focal point is established by the way the eye functions. In making the drawing, the artist does not try consciously to place the focal point, but arrives at it as a normal kinesthetic reaction to what he has seen. In the complete drawing, it is not often a definable point, as such, but comes out as a directive locus which is the key to the organization.[5] It is not usually placed on any special item of subject matter, but is built up by implication from the way in which all other space is handled. Its function is best understood in organic rather than geometric terms. When perspective (or the in-depth dimension) and composition (or the right-left, up-and-down dimensions) are made matters of special attention in a training program, the frame of reference becomes geometric, and capacity to sense the organic relativities is lost.

The effect of perceptual unity in pictorial organization is to give a drawing vitality, self-sufficiency, and integration. If the drawing is a landscape, a tree in the landscape will seem to live as it does in nature and to grow out of the soil and spot where it is placed. If the drawing is an interior, a window will stand up in its place within the walls of a room and will be felt to function as a window. It really fits into the wall, and it really admits light. If the drawing is abstract or imaginative, each form will likewise

---

[5] In the paintings of the important artists in the historical tradition, notably Rembrandt and Cézanne, the focal point as defined here is clearly demonstrable.

seem to take its rightful place and to belong just where it is. Space between the forms will give a feeling of real space. Planes, not lines, will carry the burden of the composition and perspective. All points in the picture will come up to the picture plane and be solidly set in the plane. The multi-dimensional quality of the forms as seen in the model will become transformed with authority into the two-dimensional terms of the canvas. In the words of Cézanne, the model has been "realized," or fulfilled as reality while being transferred from life to the artificial form of a drawing.

Students achieve these results without being told how to do it. They are sensitized only to the process of seeing-and-drawing, and the rest follows as a normal consequence of the approach. Had the students been told, even with great skill, the intellectual rationale of pictorial organization as they were learning it, they would not have succeeded as well as they did with their drawing. Intellectualizations would have interfered. Certainly they would not have succeeded had they been taught the clichés of geometrical perspective, dynamic symmetry, or the golden mean, which, in addition to being intellectualizations, are separated elements, severed from the living organic act, and taught as tricks of technique. The center of the students' psychological concentration would have been shifted from the emerging creative experience as focused on the model to themselves, and they would have lost their capacity for lending themselves to the creative act.

The success of these students in pictorial organization leads to the conclusion that the achievement of perceptual unity is an answer to the perspective problem, to the composition problem, and to other classical problems of technique. One cannot have the in-depth property without a satisfactory pattern solution, and indeed no partial element in the creative act can be accomplished without the achievement of all other elements simultaneously. The "aesthetic" in pictorial organization is achieved in the organic ordering of the configuration, not in its dissected and narrowly intellectualized technical construction. Any self-conscious effort that separates the aesthetic into its verbal components, such as composition, perspective, and tonality, is a sure way of destroying the desired end. Such verbalisms are suitable for certain limited purposes, but these purposes can appropriately appear only after the students are already basically self-sufficient without them.

The semi-abstract subjects in Figure 25 show that students achieve an organization of abstract forms which is comparable to the organization achieved with more naturalistic subjects.[6] These three sketches by Duncan, Adams, and Fisher were two-minute drawings of the model also presented in Figure 25 and were made from flash exposure at about the tenth training period. Despite the widely varied manner in which the original model is interpreted, the pictorial organization of each is satisfying. The handling of space and form has the same quality that appeared in later work by the students. The

[6] It is not commonly understood that the abstract paintings of Braque, Picasso, and others are well organized configurations which, like all paintings, are subject to perceptual unity. They are not simply the decorative patterns they are commonly thought to be. The dualism between abstract and realistic art, as well as many other dualisms in art, drop away when a person sees and appreciates with perceptual unity.

  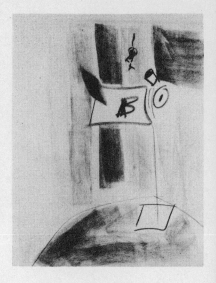

By Duncan   *By Adams*   *By Fisher*

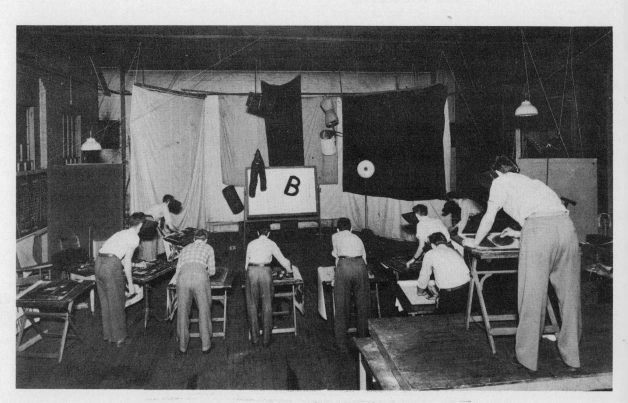

Figure 25. Drawings from suspended models with laboratory set-up.
(Note: Cardboard masks were used before total blackout facilities were available.)

Figure 26.

Drawing by Gordon from dancer.

Figure 27.

Drawing by Hawkins from dancer.

subject matter, whether abstract, imaginative, or realistic, has little effect on the success of pictorial organization, since organization depends upon the way in which the material is ordered by the artist and not upon meanings associated with the model.

The drawings by students Gordon and Hawkins in Figures 26 and 27 are included to illustrate again the variety of stylistic interpretations placed upon a similar subject by different students. The model in this case was a dancer whose movement was caught by flash exposure in the dark room. The sketches were done after about thirteen hours of training. We see in Figure 26 an interpretation which is suggestive of the primitive qualities found in the Benin bronzes of Africa and in the Bultos woodcarvings from our own Southwest. In Figure 27, there is a linear emphasis suggestive of the style found in Cretan terra cottas.

Running throughout the discussion of all these drawings has been one central principle: that perceptual unity in the seeing-and-drawing act is the first requisite to success, and that this skill having been acquired, classical problems in art performance tend to solve themselves. Style, individuality, universality, subject matter, freedom of expression, texture, composition, tonality, color, form, perspective, all are instrumental and incidental aspects of the total process, and are best handled, when teaching beginning students, by making no mention of them but by giving many exercises each of which calls for the full completion of the creative act. A repeated and deepening experience with the total organic process of seeing-and-drawing tends to take care of the details without fuss and bother, and at the same time tends to give the students the inherently rewarding effect which comes from creative expression. Later, when the students are well developed in the total act, they may practice on special techniques or become analytical and critical of their work and the work of others. Even this, however, has to be done cautiously because our culture has already infused the students with too much faith in technical and analytic manipulations, and overemphasis is easily possible after the gates have been opened to these too familiar channels. But having once realized the deeper satisfaction of creating with organic unity, the students will want more of these experiences.

Reactions of the Students

The instructor took more than a passive interest in observing the students' reactions during the program. The proper timing of events in the progressive development of the project was essential to its success. Nothing should freeze or stagnate, and each day should bring new challenges in just the right proportions to stretch experience but not to break the connecting bonds of habit. In controlling the tempo and order of events, cues from the creations of the students in the working situation were as important as the drawings. Hence the instructor tried to stay closely attuned to the students' reactions and observed carefully their facial expressions, offhand comments, questions, degree of concentration, extent of pride in work done, bodily freedom, response to the music, and the like.

40

There can be no doubt that the students as a whole greatly enjoyed the experience. At first they were curious, puzzled, and attracted by the new, experimental program—working in the dark; responding to the music; looking at abstract shapes on the screen or suspended in mid-air; moving about freely; talking and singing in class; making big, free, sweeping movements with their arms; using lots of paper, nothing precious, nothing set; moving rapidly into things they had never thought they dared to try. Later, as the problems grew in complexity and as the students' confidence and skill increased, their early curiosity about the program was supplanted by a deeper appreciation of what was happening inside themselves. Many sensations were fusing together, getting an order and finding an outlet. Their eyes, ears, hands, arms, bodies, subtle feelings inside themselves, and the world outside were working together in a harmony and freedom they had not often, if ever, experienced before. Initial curiosity about the strange program was being replaced by a deepening appreciation of themselves and the significance of the creative act.

Early in the program some of the students were suspicious of a pedagogical trick. They expected, sooner or later, to find the whole thing to be a build-up for a typical academic problem or a disguised lecture on what they should see, be, and believe. When they learned, however, that this experience was something to be taken for its own meanings, they relaxed, gave themselves to it, and accepted each hour for what it had to bring.

They were surprised to learn that they had abilities in art. Many of them had supposed that only talented persons or queer persons could be interested in or successful in the arts. However, here they were creating drawings which were creditable, fun to do, and promising of deeper things to come. "I didn't know I had this in me"; "Looks like I've been hiding my talents"; "You say this is all right even if I don't make it look like somebody else's" were comments they frequently made. Sometimes they would sit on the floor and draw like children having a good time with their toys. "Well, Doc, I used to think fishing was the only thing I could do all day long, but I think I could do this all day long, too," was the way one student put it. Sometimes, on the later and longer problems, they would forget about the bell and remain well beyond the time they were supposed to stay.

Among the twenty-five students, one, Adams, seemed to be uncomfortable during the experience. It was Adams who did the naive sketch from Pascin's "Girl Seated" (Figure 14). As long as he worked on abstract subjects he felt safe, and did well by the standards of the class, as evidenced in Figure 25, which was done in the dark with flash exposure. It was only when he worked with more familiar subjects, such as the Pascin, that he became dissatisfied. He was intellectually aware of the disproportionate size of the figure, and knew he was being naive even though he did not use (or hear) the word. His psychological and mental developments were unequal, and his subtle realization of the fact made him somewhat sensitive to the opinions he supposed others might be formulating about him. This factor, plus exciting events which were happening to him outside of class, made him want to drop the course. He is the only one, however, whose reactions tended in this direction. All the others stuck faithfully by the program, and well rewarded the instructor with their own developing faith in what was going on.

Psychologists know that enthusiasms and unexpressed "prior assumptions" of a teacher in dealing with students may be enough to affect significantly the results of any experiment conducted. It is well for the reader to remember that some such effect may have carried over into the students' reactions as reported here. However, as indicated earlier, the instructor's role had to be relatively limited and objective as required by the principles governing the whole project. His function was to keep the emphasis upon the process and not upon himself or upon the intellectualized formulation of the plan. He made himself as far as possible an incidental part of the total situation in which the students worked. Such enthusiasm as would appear should come not as a reflected radiation of the instructor's feelings, but as the normal reaction to the students' discovery and development of their creative capacities. Although contagion may account for some of the effect, it seems sounder to assume that the creative process accounted for most of the enthusiasm shown.

Novelty is also asserted to be a major factor in such experiments. The contention is made that as soon as the novelty is worn off, the level of achievement will drop. Therefore a method of teaching which, in its experimental stages, produces outstanding results, may show less outstanding results as soon as the method becomes accepted and familiar.

There can be no doubt that the students were challenged by the novelty of the program. However, the conditions of the experiment do not fit into the standard conditions under which the effects of novelty have been tested. Tests to measure those effects have usually been conducted in such a way that the persons participating in the experiment continued in the same situation for a long period of time and performed the same type of duties. In the present experiment, however, the students are placed in the novel situation for only a limited time and for a specific purpose. As soon as this purpose has been fulfilled, the students are ready to work in usual situations under normal conditions. The novel features of the program are carefully designed to move the students progressively into a pattern of behavior which fits them for familiar situations. For this reason, novelty seems to have little pertinence in the interpretation of data on the seeing-and-drawing experiment. We can safely assume that the students' level of achievement in their drawings and in optical abilities will drop little, if any, simply because the method is used repeatedly in the same institution with succeeding groups of beginning students. Results have been sustained, at any rate, with successive groups taught in this school during a period of six years.

The Visual Tests

This method of teaching drawing rests to a critical degree upon the assumption that there is an intimate relation between reactions to visual cues and behavior in drawing. By this assumption, it is logical to expect some kind of demonstrable effect to show in capacity to respond to visual cues as the drawing project progresses. If such effects are found to occur, the assumption of close relationship is substantiated.

To determine whether this assumption is true, an extensive program of testing was undertaken to check visual changes. The program was carried out in collaboration with the School of Optometry and the Department of Psychology and was itself experimental in many respects. The tests used were adapted from standard tests in these fields.

The persons selecting the tests to be used concluded that when an individual sees with perceptual unity he has a quality in his vision which may be resolved for measurement purposes into abilities to see a focal point, to see the whole field as related to the focal point, to make judgments of depth in space, and to discriminate subtle variations in tonal qualities. Translated into the language of psychology and optometry, these are abilities in *central acuity, peripheral acuity, central stereo-acuity, peripheral stereo-acuity,* and *brightness discrimination.* Tests which have been developed to measure each of these abilities were used in this program. The tests were run twice, once at the beginning of the training program and once at the end. The following paragraphs give a brief statement of the function of each test and a report on results.

The test for *central acuity* measures the degree to which the subject can perceive the form of a target placed in the center of the field of vision. Variations are measured in terms of the size of the target required in each given case. The standard of measure is the *Snellen Fraction* by which normal vision is expressed as 20/20. The numerator is a symbol for the distance between the eye of the observer and the test target, and remains at 20. The denominator is a symbol for the size of the target, and varies with the ability of the observer. Results are reported in terms of the denominator. The smaller the number, the smaller the target, and the greater the ability of the subject.

The test of *peripheral acuity* measures the degree to which the subject can perceive the form of a target which is placed at increasing distances to the right and left of the center of the field of vision. The standard of measure is the number of degrees in the angle formed by two lines, one of which extends from the eye of the subject to the center of the field, and the other from the eye to the point farthest from the center at which he can see the target. The larger the number of degrees reported, the wider the angle of vision, and the greater the ability of the subject.

The test of *central stereo-acuity* measures the degree to which the subject can make judgments of depth at the center of the field of vision. The standard of measure is the number of centimeters by which two targets must be separated before the subject notices that they are out of alignment. The smaller the number, the more precise the setting, and the greater ability of the subject.

The test of *peripheral stereo-acuity* measures the degree to which the subject can make judgments of depth at the periphery of the field of vision. The standard of measure is the same as for peripheral acuity already defined. The limit of the field of vision is set, however, as that point farthest from the center at which more than ten centimeters are needed between two targets before the subject notices that they are out of alignment. The larger the number, the wider the angle of vision, and the greater the ability of the subject.

The test of *brightness discrimination* measures the degree to which the subject can discriminate subtle shadings of light. Variations are measured in terms of the difference in light intensity at which the subject can discriminate between a spot of light and its background. The standard of measure is usually expressed in candles per square meter. In this experiment, a ten-point linear scale, starting at zero candles per square meter and ending at 0.4 candles, is used for convenience in recording and reporting results. The smaller the number, the nearer the light value of the spot to the light value of the background, and the greater the ability of the subject.

To afford a point of comparison for the test results with the experimental group, a control group, composed of students who were not involved in the training, was given four of the five tests at the same time and under the same conditions as the experimental group. There was no opportunity to measure the control group on the fifth test.

The table below presents a summary of the results. Column 2 gives the number of cases in each group; Column 3, the range of scores on the pre-test; Column 4, the average score on the pre-test; Column 5, the range of scores on the post-test; Column 6, the average score on the post-test; Column 7, the gain (or loss) between the average on the pre-test

RESULTS ON THE VISUAL TESTS							PERCENTAGE OF CHANCE (8)
		PRE-TEST		POST-TEST			
ABILITY (1)	No. (2)	Range (3)	Average (4)	Range (5)	Average (6)	GAIN (7)	
Central acuity—							
Experimental	25	38.4-15.7	22.3	26.2-11.5	18.9	3.4	0.1
Control	12	28.6-16.4	22.0	26.1-17.2	20.6	1.4	5
Peripheral acuity—							
Experimental	13	12.6-0	5.5	14.0-4.1	7.5	2.0	5
Control	10	12.5-0	6.0	12.2-1.8	6.7	0.7	50
Central stereo-acuity—							
Experimental	11	6.4-0.5	3.6	5.9-0.5	2.8	0.8	20
Control	8	3.1-0.6	1.9	6.9-0.8	3.0	—1.1	20
Peripheral stereo-acuity—							
Experimental	12	0-4	2.0	1.0-7.0	4.1	2.1	1
Control	10	0-5	2.4	1.0-8.0	3.1	0.7	20
Brightness discrimination—							
Experimental	11	7.9-4.7	6.1	6.4-4.2	5.4	0.7	10

44

and the post-test; and Column 8, the percentage chance, or the number of times in one hundred at which the gain might have been due to chance.[7]

The experimental group gained on all five tests, and gained more than the control group in all cases where there were comparisons. The gains made by the experimental group were statistically significant in central acuity, peripheral acuity, and the peripheral stereo-acuity. Chance would account for these gains less than five times in one hundred. Gains in brightness discrimination were enough to suggest a trend in the positive direction but not enough to reach a high degree of statistical reliability. Gains in central stereo-acuity were not statistically significant.

Gains made by the control group were insignificant on all tests except central acuity, indicating that practice in taking this particular test probably accounted for some of the gain in the scores of the experimental group as well. If, however, it is assumed that the gain from practice would have been the same for the experimental group as for the control group, the balance gained by the experimental group would still have been statistically significant at the 2 per cent level. In terms of individual cases, 72 per cent of the students in the experimental group exceeded the average gain of the control group. The training therefore seems to have had a significant effect in increasing central acuity. [8]

When the gain of the experimental group in peripheral acuity is expressed in terms of the area of circles within which vision was effective on the pre- and post-tests, the increase in the field of vision was 86 per cent, which means a significantly expanded visual world. Results with another experimental group of twelve students, not included in the table because a different method of testing was used and no control group was available for comparison, showed an even greater gain and a chance factor less than one in one thousand.

Gains in peripheral stereo-acuity were even more striking. The gain was 400 per cent in the area of circles within which depth judgment was effective. (See Figure 28.)

On the basis of logic and an understanding of the training program, these results are just about what one would expect. Greatest gains were made in those abilities which were exercised most during the training program, and least gains were made in those abilities which were exercised least. The teaching continually required practice in establishing a center of focus, in seeing the whole at a glance, and in drawing bold, broad patterns delineating the whole field—activities which emphasized central acuity, peripheral acuity, and peripheral stereo-acuity respectively. Comparatively little opportunity was offered for concentration on tonal variations and still fewer requirements were made for refined depth judgments of fixed points. These characteristics of the training are

---

[7] In calculating chance, the t-score formula was used. See E. F. Lindquist, *Statistical Analysis in Educational Research* (Boston: Houghton Mifflin Company, 1940), Chap. III.

[8] The gains in central and peripheral acuity are of particular interest because of a common assumption in the literature on the subject that central acuity can be little affected by training of any kind, and peripheral acuity only a little more. These data challenge further investigation of this common assumption.

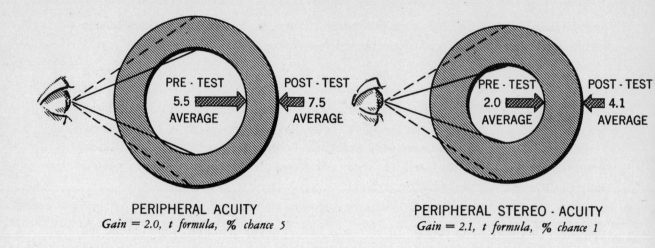

PERIPHERAL ACUITY
Gain = 2.0, t formula, % chance 5

PERIPHERAL STEREO - ACUITY
Gain = 2.1, t formula, % chance 1

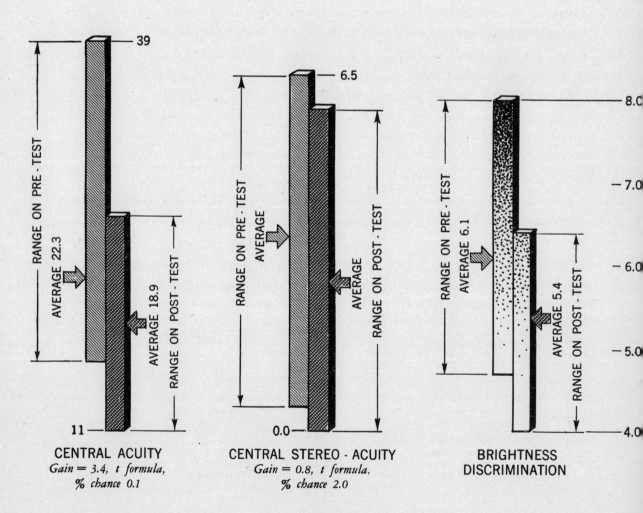

CENTRAL ACUITY
Gain = 3.4, t formula,
% chance 0.1

CENTRAL STEREO - ACUITY
Gain = 0.8, t formula,
% chance 2.0

BRIGHTNESS
DISCRIMINATION

Figure 28.

reflected in the results on the tests of brightness discrimination and central stereo-acuity respectively.

The evidence is clear, then, that the kind of training in drawing which was used in this experiment was also a training in seeing, and that as the ability in drawing developed, ability in seeing developed, particularly at the points where the most practice was required.[9]

We doubt that just any kind of training in drawing and painting would bring these results. We do hold the view, however, that the most effective programs in drawing and painting will show changes in eye behavior. A training program in arts which goes deep enough to establish fresh abilities in seeing is also likely to go deep enough to open up channels of ready action throughout all of the student's behavior so that he has much more fluid power for expressing himself. The drawings and paintings of the students in this experiment showed unusual improvement in their capacities to express themselves, thus substantiating the hypotheses on which the project was based.

While the number of cases was small and the results must be taken tentatively, the weight of the evidence thus far clearly supports the concept of perceptual unity in one of its basic tenets that training in drawing involves also training in seeing. Instead of using the phrase "beginning drawing" to describe the early work of students in the visual arts, the profession should prefer to use "beginning seeing-and-drawing," since the two are as one within the process by which drawings and paintings of quality are most efficiently created.

Summary Interpretation of Results of the Teaching Method

Evidence has been presented from the drawings of the students, from their reactions to the experience, and from visual tests. At all points along the line, the trend supports the concept of perceptual unity as an effective guide to teaching drawing. The central principle is that success in drawing depends upon the process of seeing-and-drawing with perceptual unity—i.e., a person must see all points in a model with relation to a focal point, and must be disciplined to allow the image, so perceived, to form itself through kinesthetic and related channels into the eventual drawing.

When teaching of beginning students was done with this principle as the key to all operations, the following things happened:

1. Drawings and paintings achieved vitality, self-sufficiency, integration, and an unusual degree of satisfying pictorial organization.

2. These results were achieved in fifteen to twenty hours of training time.

---

[9] This inter-effect of improvement in drawing on improvement in seeing must not, however, unwittingly be interpreted to mean that high scores on the tests necessarily mean high creative ability in the visual arts. Much more is involved in creative drawing than just seeing. Those students in the experiment (Brown and Evans are examples) who had high scores on one or more of the tests, or who showed marked improvement in some of their scores, did the most outstanding creative work, but the creative work was dependent on psychological, kinesthetic, tactile, and other abilities as well as visual abilities. The tests are visual tests, not tests of creative ability, and are therefore to be used simply as indicators of what has been done or might be done through a training program to reach students at a fundamental level.

3. Average students did creative work. Neither talent, prior training, nor an expressed interest in the arts were prerequisites.

4. Classical problems in art teaching tended to solve themselves. Reacting in terms of the "whole," the students handled the "parts."

> a. Style disappeared as a special problem; it was achieved as an incidental aspect of the total creative act.

> b. Subject-matter disappeared as a special problem; all forms were handled by the same visual principles, regardless of the nature of the subject matter.

> c. Texture disappeared as a special problem; charcoal, brush, and paint were manipulated for textural effects as a normal fulfillment of the total creative act.

> d. Perspective disappeared as a special problem; as but one of the many dimensions with which the students saw-and-drew, perspective was handled as an incidental matter.

> e. Composition disappeared as a special problem; like perspective, it disappeared because it covers but one range of dimensions and the students were seeing-and-drawing in terms of many dimensions.

> f. Value disappeared as a special problem; tonality was achieved as a normal aspect of fulfilling the total creative act.

> g. Color disappeared as a special problem; color was treated as a function of form and was handled in the same manner as other problems of form.

> h. The above-mentioned and other classical problems of technique came to be handled as instrumental and incidental aspects of the total, on-going process, the power of which supplied, without waste and misemphasis, the free-flowing means to achieve partial elements which have historically been abstracted for labored and mistaken special treatment.

6. Basic training was given for painting at the same time it was given for drawing. Operational understandings were achieved at a deep enough level to make transfer from one medium to another a matter of course.

7. Students enjoyed the experience; individual personalities had an opportunity for expression; heretofore unknown abilities were discovered and developed; integration of optical, auditory, kinesthetic, motor, tactile, psychological, and intellectual sensations was stimulated; the drawing act, as a creative act, came to have recreational value and was appreciated for its own sake.

8. Visual abilities improved; students were able to see in a wider visual field and to see more within the field.

These results on the first two groups of students point collectively and consistently to the validity of the methods used. The number of cases in these groups total but twenty-five, and it has not been possible to assemble and analyze in such detail the results which have been obtained with subsequent groups. Hence, there is need for more experimental evidence before all the elements in the program are adequately tested. Experience with subsequent groups, however, has raised no challenge to the findings reported here, and has deepened our conviction as to the soundness of the program.

Faith in the program, at any rate, does not and need not derive solely from experimental results at this stage of development. Throughout the study, as discussion has penetrated particular points, as rationale has developed, and as principles have emerged, the concept has gained the support of its own internal logical and psychological consistency. Each point has tended to augment, amplify, and support each other point; and the deeper analysis has gone, the more penetrating and wider the meanings of the concept have become.

Furthermore, while the concept is resolving many of the traditional problems in art teaching, it is also harmonizing with conceptions now current in other fields—education, psychology, biology, semantics, science, and mathematics. "Relativity" stands at the heart of this point of view as does "Gestalt," "functionalism," "organismic behavior," concepts which describe the intellectual formulations of this cultural period. Validity stems from harmonizing support of these notions which in their own fields are proving to be good assumptions for solving the problems of the various professions to which they are applied.

It is not accidental that the concept of perceptual unity can be stated in the twentieth century and could not well have been stated earlier. The times require it and give it birth, opening a way by which art and art education may more readily be re-united with other elements in the culture and be integrated more successfully into the living of the people. This carries us to the more detailed and systematic consideration of the implications of the concept for art and art education as well as for other fields in which visual and creative capacities are required.

Chapter Five

IMPLICATIONS AND APPLICATIONS

TO REVIEW the course of the discussion thus far, the preceding chapters have (1) told how the concept of perceptual unity developed and how it came to be used as a guide to the development of a teaching program, (2) presented the basic principles in the concept and the ways by which these principles led to particular methods in the classroom, (3) described the classroom procedures, and (4) analyzed results which have come from research on early experimental groups.

This chapter presents some deductions as to what can happen if the concept of perceptual unity is accepted and applied. By showing what its potential application to practical problems may mean, the significance of the concept can be better appraised. At the same time, suggestions are made which may serve as guides to further thinking and research. Each point is to be taken as a hypothesis rather than as a conclusion reached on the basis of the limited data presented in the preceding pages. In our opinion, each suggestion is sufficiently substantiated by data and by logic to merit serious consideration.

The discussion falls into two parts, the first presenting implications of the concept and teaching method for art and art education, and the second presenting applications to related fields which are dependent on visual skills.

Implications for Art and Art Education

The concept of perceptual unity means for art and art education that:

1. *The time allotted for teaching beginning drawing can be greatly reduced.* Effective results can be obtained in fifteen to twenty hours of training time. The length of the program can be reduced from the usual twelve or eighteen weeks to six weeks; the laboratory period can be reduced from the customary two or three hours to an average of less than an hour. The time saved can be used by the staff for teaching a larger number of students and by the students for advanced work or courses in other areas.

2. *The number of students can be greatly increased.* Many students who would not be interested in beginning drawing, as it is usually taught, can easily become interested in the course when it is taught by the methods of perceptual unity. The methods are in such

contrast with those used in any other courses that the experience is something which many students will want for its own sake. This motive is enough since the evidence indicates that students picked at random can do very good work if they are simply willing to lend themselves for a short time to a fresh experience. The door can therefore be opened to all students and not be limited merely to those who feel they have a special interest or talent in the arts. Many, who would not dare to think of themselves as potential artists, are nevertheless seeking creative experiences and opportunities for self-expression, and will enroll when they understand that the beginning drawing class may be taken for these purposes.

3. *Important services can be offered to students in many fields of study.* Since the course is as much a training in seeing as it is a training in drawing, it can serve students in many areas of activity other than the area of fine arts. Seeing with perceptual unity, or the ability to see the whole at a glance, can add efficiency to the performance of students in such common activities as reading and athletics, and in the occupations of architecture, engineering design, landscape architecture, floriculture, photography, interior decorating, window trimming, advertising, music, optometry, surgery, dentistry, newspaper and scientific reporting, and indeed wherever the eyes perform an analytical and evaluative function. This assumes that the ability to see with perceptual unity transfers from the drawing laboratory to these related activities. Data on this assumption have not yet been formally collected, but such as have been collected informally, and certainly the logic of the case, point clearly to the ability of students to see the whole in whatever they look at, whether it be a model in the studio, a page of print, a landscape design, a bouquet of flowers, a store window, or a street accident. Possibilities for research regarding such applications are treated in some detail in the later pages of this chapter.

4. *Indispensable experiences can be provided to beginning students in all branches of the visual arts.* All branches of the visual arts — drawing, design, painting, ceramics, and sculpture — obviously depend to a critical degree on visual forms and on creative kin-esthetic reactions to these forms. Anything which helps students to develop rapidly their abilities to perceive visual relationships and to react creatively is of fundamental importance to all these branches of art. The course in drawing performs these functions efficiently. It is well suited as a basic first course for students in all branches. In taking the course, students can come to see that the various media used in the different fields are instruments only, and that a common process binds them all together. They become aware that the evidences of process in any art product are the important qualities, whatever the medium used. A way is opened for destroying some of the artificial and pedantic barriers which too often appear in art departments.

5. *A good foundation can be provided for art appreciation.* Of the various elements which may be involved in the appreciation of art, the most critical is that of experiencing the process of creating. When a person has this experience, he has something in terms

of which the art creations of others can come to be felt and interpreted; without it, he gets little from his struggle to put meaning into what he sees. Of almost equal importance, because many of the arts are visual, is his capacity to see with perceptual unity. If he has a sense for visual relationships, he has a way of focusing his reactions against the visual pattern of what he sees. These elements, the creative experience and the ability to see with perceptual unity, are dominant in the beginning drawing course, making it a fertile first experience for later courses in the appreciation of art. For students who go no further in the fine arts, this training might well be used as the initial unit in an art-appreciation course. No better use could be made of the time in the first weeks.

Without a creative experience and ability to see with unity, students are inclined to center their thinking on the styles in art rather than on the art process. The result is that their appreciation is superficial and is artificially limited to a few styles which they defensively claim they "like." Such attitudes foster the notion that each style is a class by itself, is good or bad in itself, and is subject to its own laws. Barriers developed among the styles are effective in preventing students from getting from art a range of values which they might otherwise obtain.

Students who are trained in the process of perceptual unity, however, avoid these barriers. Within their own classroom they see themselves and their friends turning out drawings which have the flavor of the primitive, the sophisticated, the abstract, the naturalistic, and other typical styles. Each style comes to be recognized and accepted as an extension of a relative phase of personal or cultural expression rather than as an absolute category to be treated as something in itself. The doors are therefore opened for them to get something from every style and to appreciate the fundamental significance of a very wide range of artistic expressions.

The history of art also has more significance. The function of history is not to present the dates which separate one event from another, but to present past human experiences in such a way as to allow them to be re-experienced in the present. Students should come to the art works of the past with the same expectancy and sensitivity with which they approach immediate situations for a creative experience. Training in the process of perceptual unity aids this approach. Being made capable of art experience in their own work, they are better able to absorb the harmonies of creative experiencing which exude from the art works of others. The life of humanity is better able to strike a resonant chord in the life of the individual student and to lend him the supporting strength which contact with universals allows. Within this experience, the accompanying rationale, which presents the organic order in which cultures and individuals have come to their expressions, can take on immediate meaning, and can illuminate the path by which the student, too, is developing and may develop further into a more significant human being. He is better able to feel himself as a part of history and history as being recreated in him. Under these circumstances, the history of art can come to be a more vitalizing subject than it usually is.

52

6. *Standards can be established for art criticism.* The concept of perceptual unity establishes one central principle by which all works of art can be judged, i.e., the principle of perceptual unity. It is perfectly clear that drawings and paintings which do not have perceptual unity have little chance of being works of sustained value. The painters whose works have been selected through the ages and called great are painters who were able to achieve perceptual unity. This kind of unity is not a technique but a concrete record of a creative and integrated experience which the painter is able to record through his brush. His painting is thereafter valuable to other people because it stirs them in turn to a creative experience. Perceptual unity is the medium whereby the creative experience of the painter is communicated to the onlooker. The creative experience is what human beings prize most in their art.

Some critics have realized this point and have tried very hard to find some way of saying what they mean.[1] The best they have been able to do has been to repeat some such phrase as, "a good work of art has a unity which is like that of a living organism; this painting does (or does not) have this kind of unity." If they attempt to go further, they talk in further figures of speech or pick out details which seem to illustrate what they feel, thus getting around their subject but not into it. They are able to recognize when the organism is living, so to speak, but are not able to point out the ways by which the organism comes to be living. The concept of perceptual unity, in showing the conditions under which a painting comes to have unity, illuminates the process and gives the art critic a much more effective guide to his criticism. He has a rationale and a way of better explaining what he means and of better selecting the kinds of things which are pertinent to say.

Many critics, unfortunately, have not realized the point about unity and, in their search for something to say, have gone off into long descriptions of techniques, styles, ways of getting special effects, etc., which are misleading and dangerous. Such talk encourages readers to assume that the painter who is successful is the man who is smart in handling his techniques, that painting is just a technical problem. Consequently, students who have sought to achieve what the masters achieved have been tempted to dabble around with devices and schemes, instead of putting themselves in position to be the instrument which, through painting, records a creative experience. The concept of perceptual unity should make it easier to eradicate this kind of art criticism.

7. *A gap can be filled in our pattern of education.* In our program of education in America we tend to give very few opportunities for creative experience to the majority of students. This is a danger to our culture when considered in conjunction with our tendency to give too great importance to the ego and the intellect. Students are unwittingly taught to believe that human beings can do almost anything they want if they know what they want and do a smart job of planning to get it. This is part of the American dream and a natural result of our outstanding success in conquering a continent

---

[1] Among these critics are Leo Stein, Roger Fry, Herbert Reed.

and getting its material goods in order. The dream is reflected in our pattern of education in that most college courses are taught so that students get ahead if they can learn how to manipulate a body of knowledge about things "out there." The danger in this is that the students fail to take into account the world which lies within them and the ways in which they can achieve health and happiness by harmonizing themselves with the universe rather than by trying to rule it. Creative experiences can teach these balancing lessons.

In the training course in drawing, the students can learn how it is that some of the most valuable things in life come, not by deciding what to do and doing it, but by relaxing the ego and letting things come out of the center of oneself as they will. They learn that one doesn't get a drawing of much value by deciding what to put on a piece of paper and trying to put it there. Rather one subdues that deciding mechanism and lets *himself* go, while responding to a concourse of kinesthetic, tactile, psychological, auditory, and optical sensations which somehow take order without the ego being there to boss it. They discover a new center of focus in themselves which allows all of themselves to blend in a harmonious relation with the universe around them. They begin to marvel at the unknown things they have within them, and to respect what has been given them without their having done much to put it there. They sense that what comes out of life is dependent on the things which are given as well as upon the things one can reach for and get, and that there is a special kind of happiness which comes when a harmony is established among the many parts of oneself and between oneself and the universe. A gap in their education can be filled, and something learned which, in this century, may be quite as important for Americans to know as, a century ago, it was important to know that great things could be done if one simply knew what he wanted and went out to make the world give it to him.

Applications to Related Fields

The concept of perceptual unity, when applied with necessary adaptations, offers possibilities for developments of importance in these fields:

1. *Optometry and the psychology of vision.* The data on the visual tests, as reported in preceding pages, indicate that the training in drawing produced significant improvement in the capacity of the eyes to see in broader fields of vision and to see more effectively within these fields. The training program was not directed toward the achievement of these results but nevertheless accomplished significant improvements. This suggests the hypothesis that an efficient way to improve visual capacities is to arrange situations which will require the eye to function as one organism among many in an integrative and creative experience. Optometrists and psychologists have usually worked on vision as a separated segment of human activity. Thus far, improvement in visual capacities has been attempted through exercises for the eye as an independent organism. Perhaps an approach in terms of the "whole" will prove more efficient than an approach in terms of the "parts." Promising research possibilities are indicated.

54

2. *Clinical psychology.* Clinical psychologists and psychiatrists have used drawing and painting for their therapeutic value and as a means of getting evidence on the "unconscious." They have had to develop their own approach to creative work without aid or understanding from many professional artists. Training by the methods of perceptual unity, however, offers an opportunity for clinical psychologists and artists to combine their research in this field. Therapeutic effects are doubtless derived. The possibilities of diagnosis appear to be rich, for the procedure allows unconscious elements in the personality of a student to appear in his drawings. The drawings obtained from the students in our demonstration showed great variety in this respect. Clinical psychologists may study the relation between such drawings and personality. Two important possibilities are the development of a maturity scale and the investigation of the degree to which the "collective unconscious" appears to be active in normal persons. A drawing laboratory would offer an opportunity for the study of normal cases under favorable conditions which are not often allowed to clinical psychologists who usually deal with abnormal cases in unnatural surroundings.

2. *Educational psychology.* While the experimental program described in this report was set up primarily in terms of training in art, it is equally an experiment in educational psychology. Many of the classical problems in the psychology of education lie at the heart of the experiment and are met with positive solutions. Gestalt concepts dominate the pattern. Learning is required in terms of the whole, is functional, dynamic, organic, integrative. Individual differences are respected, and are treated as scientific necessities for the learning act. The role of the teacher is defined as that of arranging situations for the development of the central process in the students, not that of dominating the classroom with his dogma or his personality. Methods of teaching the creative act are demonstrated. The curriculum is ordered organically. The results are clear in both qualitative and quantitative respects. A concrete, clear, organically unified, and well-defined situation is presented for research—a rare opportunity in the complex field of educational psychology.

4. *Therapy and rehabilitation.* The training program as described here is practical and potentially valuable for therapy in military and other hospitals. It does what mass therapy projects are supposed to do. It is entertaining, has novelty, uncovers unsuspected talents in the average man, allows for personal expression, and develops a sense of integration. The program is brief, materials are relatively inexpensive, and patients who can complete the program are sufficiently independent to go ahead with drawing and painting for their own pleasure.[2]

---

[2] For certain kinds of cases, the training may have special significance. For example, the near blind may be taught to use what vision they have with increased efficiency. The training would help them get the habit of seeing the whole field, of retaining the image seen for a longer time, of noting objects in the field with greater accuracy, of reacting more quickly and confidently. Being based on an integration of the seeing act with tactile and kinesthetic response, the training program is of a nature to take advantage of the tactile and kinesthetic sensitivity of the near blind and to bring these powers into the stream of influences contributing to the retraining of sight.

5. *Aviation.* Seeing from a free-moving body in the air is quite different from seeing from a fixed or moving point on the ground. Customary associations for judging distances are lacking. Only a few, subtle, and frequently moving reference points are available for estimating distance. There is an unusual requirement for taking the "whole field" into account and for basing judgments on constantly changing spatial relations. At the same time, the kinesthetic action in manipulating the airplane needs to be quick, accurate, and sure in response to the optical judgments made. Night flying poses new problems in judging all these relationships in the low value scale. These are well-known, crucial problems in aviation. The training in drawing with perceptual unity develops many of the particular abilities required — reacting in terms of the whole, taking all reference points as relative, working in the dark and with slight nuances of value, reacting quickly and confidently in kinesthetic terms. For both testing and training of pilots, the program may well have cogent meaning.[3]

6. *Architecture and landscape architecture.* Many architects tend to be harnessed by set formulas for design which are based upon the principle of building up the whole from the parts. The result is that their building and landscape arrangements seldom attain a satisfying unity and often seem divorced from the setting. A training for architects which would provide practice in visualizing the whole as a whole and which would open up new procedures for interpreting the possibilities of materials in terms of their function within the whole could contribute greatly to the improvement of architecture. The training course in drawing might well be a good place to start.

7. *Athletics and physical education.* Most sports—notably football, basketball, baseball, hockey, soccer, tennis, and handball—require a high degree of visual skill if competency is to be achieved in the sport. The good player must be able to see the whole visual field in which the play is emerging, and he must see most of it as peripheral vision, out of the corner of his eye. Judgments within the field also have to be accurate since he may have to whirl and catch the ball, intercept the runner, and so on. The training in drawing increased the field of peripheral vision of students in this demonstration by 86 per cent and increased the accuracy of depth judgments in the periphery

---

[3] One of the most common difficulties in learning to draw is learning how to deal with the foreground plane. This difficulty was met in a highly satisfactory way by the students in this experiment. Success is believed to result from their training to see with perceptual unity and from that part of the training which gave special emphasis to drawing from the "flashed" horizontal plane. There is every reason to believe that this phase of the training might be developed to train depth perception of the horizontal plane. This would have direct application to the aircraft landing problem, particularly the problem of night landings on carriers where the spatial judgment of the flight deck at low visual thresholds is a critical one.

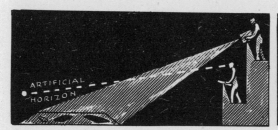 

by 400 per cent. There was also constant practice in reacting instantly and boldly to the images seen. This suggests that a similar or adapted program might be used both for selecting and training skilled athletes.

8. *Surgery and dentistry.* The fine arts are not the only fields in which the stroke of the hand has to be quick and sure and properly placed with relation to surrounding objects. Surgery and dentistry are fields in which the skill has to be highly developed, and in which the consequences of any clumsiness are much more important than they are in the fine arts. How surgeons and dentists are trained to take into account the visual field in which they have to work and to place their strokes in deft relation to what they see is of utmost importance. Indications are that comparatively little attention is given to the methods of training which are used on this point. It is not hard to believe that when men become efficient in these fields they are artists and that their modes of reaction have to be those of the artistic process. The process might be called seeing-and-cutting instead of seeing-and-drawing, but the essentials are the same. All this suggests that the drawing program can have considerable significance in these fields, both directly for training the students and indirectly for pointing to the kinds of things which need to be taken into account when adapting the program to the particular problems of the surgeon and dentist.[4]

9. *Music.* One of the knotty problems in music education is learning to read music in terms of phrases instead of individual notes, and, of course, to react kinesthetically so as to play the right notes at the right time. It is seeing-and-playing instead of seeing-and-drawing, a suggestion which carries with it the prospect of considerably altered methods of teaching beginning music. For the present, however, the training in drawing might solve with greater efficiency than any other method now known, the problem of teaching students to see whole phrases instead of individual notes and to hold the image until the kinesthetic reactions are completed. Some significant values can certainly be obtained.

10. *Reading.* Many readers are slow because they read words instead of lines and paragraphs. Experimentation has already been done in the field to show that it is possible to read by lines and paragraphs if the eyes are properly trained. The program offered in drawing may prove to be an effective method for teaching the desired skill in reading. Though reading does not require a kinesthetic type of creative reaction in the same sense

---

[4] Since this chapter was written, a project for training dental students has been undertaken. The opportunities for adaptation of the process to the special problems of dentistry are many. As examples, "A" shows a slide problem for drawing; "B," a slide problem for modeling in clay; "C," a slide problem for carving in plaster; and "D," a slide problem for cutting, punching, and filing metal. All problems are done from flash and in the dark.

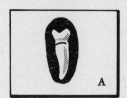   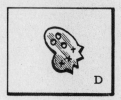

that drawing does, it may well be that the experience in seeing-and-drawing would carry more power for developing the ability to see lines and paragraphs than direct training of the eyes on reading because, in the seeing-and-drawing process, more of the body is involved. There are more connections to the behavior of the eye and for that reason the training of the eye may be more efficiently done by means of the drawing. The transfer to the particulars of the reading problem may take less energy than would be required to train the eyes directly. There is good ground for this hypothesis.

11. *General education.* As already apparent in the many lines of application indicated above, the training in drawing might well be considered a basic element in general education. The degree to which, and the ways in which, the training as given may successfully affect behavior in these related fields will not be determined until experiments are made. However, the problem of transfer which is at the heart of the problem of general education and which hit a snag in the specifics doctrine of behaviorism may have come much nearer solution in terms of Gestalt principles. It may be that a program of seeing-and-drawing has significant transfer to any other type of behavior to which the phrase "seeing-and————" can be applied such as, seeing-and-reading, seeing-and-playing (music), and seeing-and-catching, -dodging, or -hitting (athletics). Some students who have taken the course have come to the instructor to express their appreciation for the course in terms of what they consider to be transfer of skill from seeing-and-drawing to more rapid reading, more accurate baseball pitching, more freedom of movement and comprehension in playing music, and even better organized and more flexible thinking.

Whether or not the transfer to other areas proves to be of great significance, there remain the fundamental values of the course itself: a realization of new abilities, an appreciation of visual forms, a sense for the processes of art, a background of vital experience for further courses in art, a taste of the kind of freedom which comes from creative experience, and an introduction of the students to new worlds within themselves and new relationships between themselves and the universe. These are the values sought in a program of rounded, general education, and, regardless of the amount of transfer of skill, such values are sufficient to justify the use of the course in a general education curriculum.

Thus the concept of perceptual unity and the teaching method to which it leads have implications and applications in many directions beyond the teaching of beginning drawing. Further projects are indicated. In due time the full significance of the concept can be better realized, tested, and defined.[5]

---

[5] Possibilities of application of the training program to other fields are continually opening up. Two such areas have recently been suggested and partially developed.
Advertising layout: Those who are successful in advertising layout must have a well-developed sense for the pattern which immediately centers the attention of the eye and gives, at a glance, the whole effect desired. This calls for an operational understanding of the role played by position, size, and brightness in creating visual effects. The training program with the spot slides, supplemented by slides adapted to the particulars of layout problems, is well suited to the development of this ability. Samples below suggest the character of the slides adapted to the layout problem. An evening school group in advertising has recently experimented with the program and has been well satisfied with the results.

Perceptual unity fits into a stream of progressive developments, starting with Masaccio in the 15th Century, and developing, spiral-like, ever since. Skilled artists have drawn with perceptual unity, but without full awareness of what they were doing. They were interested in the end-product more than they were in the behavioristic processes by which good painting was achieved. Our age, however, always interested in the pragmatic question of how things are done, has forced attention to the process, and thereby has opened up a new channel of understanding. The result seems to be that the average person may now have available to him a way of learning which will enable him to see with a kind of unity that formerly was possible to only a few uniquely sensitive and talented persons, such as Rembrandt and Cézanne.

Strong support of the concept comes from the fact that such ideas are everywhere in the air. The time has come in our culture when integrations of all kinds must take place. Fortunately these integrations are occurring with increased frequency because our science is becoming more mature. For many decades science was primarily involved in dividing things up and putting names on them. Now it has progressed to the point where its own fulfillment requires the relating of many parts together in active processes, thus causing the establishment of new focal points in thinking around such words as relativity, dynamics, and organic integration. The sciences are coming together inside themselves and in relation to each other. Being in this state, they are contagious for art, which is primarily integrative and dynamic in character.

One will note in this demonstration that much dependence has been placed on participation by the sciences — by optometry and psychology most directly, but by other sciences as well. The project was conducted under the auspices of a bureau of educational research, hardly a traditional place for an artist to be! Contributing directly and indirectly to the evolution of the idea were specialists in the classics, history, language, education, geology, law, journalism, dentistry, music, athletics, and military science. Although their fields are widely varied, these contributors nourished the evolution of the concept and, in return, were enabled to apply its significant principles to their own enterprises.

Lettering: The problem of lettering is closely associated with advertising layout. One of the major problems here is to get the student to compose with the letters and not just make a perfect letter. This means learning to organize with words, or "visual phrasing." The training program readily lends itself to presenting the variety of letter styles by the flashing of words and the subsequent execution in the dark. This would serve to emphasize the shape character of the individual letter by the way it organizes in the word. Spacing and character of shape would be integrated. This procedure would be particularly effective in free brush lettering where the execution must be generalized to be free.

The function of the concept is integration all along the line: in the composition of drawings (where it started), in the act of seeing-and-drawing, in the process of teaching, in the personality of the student, in the curriculum of the fine arts, in the pattern of general education, in the occupations dependent upon visual and artistic skills, in the intellectual formulations of the sciences, and in the union of the sciences and the arts. To show the concept of perceptual unity as it has evolved in relation to these foci of integration has been the purpose of this book, as has been also the delineation of its practical implications for quite concrete changes in the way many common activities of daily life are carried on.

APPENDICES

Appendix A

POINTERS ON CLASSROOM MANAGEMENT AND EQUIPMENT

FOR THOSE teachers who are interested in setting up a program for teaching beginning drawing in the manner described in the preceding pages, a few pointers on managing the classroom and organizing equipment may be helpful:

Classroom Management

Most essential, of course, is a full grasp of the principles and procedures described in Chapters Two and Three. Many points which may be unclear about the procedures will clear up rapidly once the teacher gets into the actual operation of the program. Provided the concept is understood and used as a basis for thinking things through, individual variations in procedure, which may lead to a few mistakes in the beginning, can in the long run serve only to enrich the program rather than to weaken it. Below are listed various time-saving devices and ways of avoiding confusion which we found helpful in the course of our experiments.

During the periods of work with lantern slides, careful attention should be given to anything which might interrupt the smooth rhythm of seeing-and-drawing. Any slight delay or off-timing is irritating. Before class begins, the students should check to see that the paper on their drawing tables is firmly fastened at the top so that the sheets will not fall out when they are turned in the dark. They should also select a suitable piece of chalk with a broad drawing surface, one that feels right to them as they begin to draw. The slides should be carefully arranged in sequence so that there is no fumbling. The phonograph records should be conveniently at hand, selected ahead of time, and changed on the machine without confusion. The key for shifting to the next slide in a series is the rustling of the papers as the students turn them in the dark; any delay at this point may cause the students to get out of the seeing-and-drawing rhythm and to fumble in getting back.

Working with chalk in the dark can be a dirty business: let the students wear smocks; give them time to clean up after class.

Avoid strain and tenseness; be relaxed and free and help the students to feel the same way. During the few minutes at the opening of the class period when the students are waiting for their eyes to become dark-adapted, start the music, let them hum and sing and feel the music in their muscles; let them talk chit-chat, encourage them to drop all thought of academic problems which they may have carried into class from a preceding subject, and avoid serious discussions or strenuous expressions of any kind. While the students are busily at work in their drawing, remind them frequently to avoid trying too hard, to stay relaxed, and to let things come out from their bodies, not from their heads. Be casual, but not indifferent. All this is part of the discipline of drawing. Each teacher will need to find his own way of developing this kind of rapport.

In the matter of music, let the students pick the kind of music they want and bring their own records to class if they like. They will differ among themselves as to the records they want played—some will want popular and some classical—but whether one or another type of music is used makes little difference in the drawing act so long as the students find the music pleasing as music. Students will report when a selection has the tempo they like best, and will object if the tempo is too slow or too fast to synchronize with their feelings as they draw. Trust their judgment.

In the beginning of the program, scrupulously avoid any situations which might lead the students to compare any drawings they are making with some standard. Not until about the third week should the slides which have been used during a given class period be run through for review at the close of the period. When these reviews are started, make them rapid and casual and tell the students to check for over-all pattern rather than for accuracy in detail. At no time during the program should there be comparison of one student's work with another's, unless it be as a matter of passing and curious interest, never as a matter of deliberate evaluation and comparison.

Don't overcrowd the classroom; there should be ample space to move the drawing tables to left and right and forward toward the screen. The classroom should suggest freedom of movement in the way it is furnished and used.

Be sure the room is completely blacked out; any stray thread of light is quite distracting and can easily blot out images seen with perceptual unity. Be sure the projector is completely boxed up so there is no leakage of light when the slide is flashed. When flood lamps are used for flash effects, use bulbs in which the afterglow dies out as quickly as possible. Photographic floodlights are better than the usual bulbs used in flood lamps because of a shorter afterglow.

Buy paper and materials which are economical and then be very free in their use. Don't be stingy; don't do anything which might cause students to feel that the instruments they are using are to be treated with special respect. It cramps their expression and misplaces the emphasis.[1]

---

[1] After considerable experimentation with varieties of black crayon, we have found "Freeart Black Crayon," manufactured by the American Crayon Company, Sandusky, Ohio, the most satisfactory. Newsprint, 18 inches by 24 inches, purchased in bulk, is the paper used in drawing.

If possible, visit a classroom where the method is being used and where the teacher is experienced enough to be confident in his procedures. A few hours spent in this way can teach a great deal which a written report cannot convey. Best of all, go through the process as a student until the point of view, the method, and the overtones are absorbed as a habitual attitude and a familiar pattern of activities.

Equipment

When work was begun at Ohio State University with the flash procedure, we had very modest equipment, and other schools will find that they can begin their programs with very little expense beyond the equipment they already have. If a totally darkened room is not immediately available, shields similar to those illustrated in Figure 29 can be made with string and black cardboard. The function of the shields is to prevent the students from seeing their drawings while working on them.

Figure 29.

Any 500-watt projector is adequate. A tachistoscope attachment can be added by purchasing a clock-motor (e.g., "Telechron"), and fitting onto the spindle a cardboard disc with one-tenth of its area removed so that, as the disc rotates, the image from the slide will be exposed for one-tenth of a second. The clock-motor with disc can be easily attached to the front of the projector in such a position as to allow the disc to rotate in front of the mouth of the projector. Any portable phonograph, placed conveniently near the projector, is suitable as a source for music. Students are glad to supply the records.

Slides can be made by working from the samples illustrated in Figures 7, 8, 9, and 10. Slides emphasizing position should number about one hundred for use during the first five class sessions. Slides including size variations should also number about one hundred for the next five class sessions. Two hundred more slides, including variations in brightness as well as size and position, are needed for the remaining ten class sessions. Once a teacher gets into the program, he will soon sense the range of possibilities in slide forms. Drawing the slides can most conveniently be done by working directly on commercially prepared cellophane sheets enclosed in carbon paper (e.g., "Radio-Mat") and mounted between two glass covers.

The screen assembly, as shown in Figure 6, can be made by sewing muslin to the appropriate size for the screens. A red spotlight can be made by taping a red gelatin covering over the mouth of a flashlight. Floodlights can be obtained at small expense from stores selling photographic equipment; the cardboard assemblies for photo flood lamps are suitable. Material for the three-dimensional problems can be taken from odds and ends around the school: wastepaper baskets, sheets of wallboard, old curtains, etc.

—anything to give variety in size and brightness when arranged in "abstract" patterns. Suspension of some of the objects from the ceiling is helpful in getting the sense of form abstraction.

With this kind of equipment, a teacher can get along very well. We have gone ahead to design a more efficient projector and record-playing assembly because we are required to service several classes a day. The assembly, illustrated in Figure 30, is built from easily available materials, and may be found useful in other centers where a large number of students need to be accommodated. The masking case of the projector (1) is of plywood construction with a small opening in front suitable for projection and a curtained opening in the back allowing easy access to the projector in operating the slides. The fixation spotlight (2) is puppet-stage type, 100 watt. The case is taped with friction tape to prevent light leakage. The projection aperture is reduced in size with tape and covered with several layers of red gelatin to create a small red fixation point. The spotlight hanger which is mounted upside down, makes an effective swivel and affords a flexible fixation point. The shutter (3) is a black cardboard disc from which is removed a segment one-tenth the circumference in size. This disc is mounted on the shutter motor spindle. The shutter motor (4) is of the clock-motor type, making one revolution per second. Thus the removed one-tenth segment creates approximately a one-tenth second exposure. The motor specifications are Type B-3-110 V. 60 cycles, manufactured by the Warren Telechron Company. Any type of 500 watt slide projector (5) is adequate.

At the start of the period the shutter switch (6) is snapped on. The fixation point button (8) is then given a short punch to get the students to fixate on the center of the screen. A signal is given the students and the projector lamp switch (7) is snapped on and off with an interval sufficient to permit the rotary shutter to make one exposure.

The flash floodlight is made of a metal hood (9) with four photo floodlights wired in parallel. The amount of light can be controlled by the number of bulbs used. For illumination during the dark-adaptation period, a red light is set in the ceiling over the drawing stands. This light (10) is the regular darkroom lamp used in photography. It proves to be a convenience when students drop their chalk, run out of paper, or otherwise need to locate an object during the blackout period.

The masking curtain (11) on the rear of the projector case provides easy access to the projector whenever it becomes necessary to make mechanical adjustments. The curtain is fastened to the underside of the hinged top. The record player (12) is a standard motor-driven turntable. The volume control knob (13) is so placed as to be most convenient to the instructor when he reduces the volume at the time for the ready-signal and when he wishes to vary the volume for special effects. On the panel below the record player are four toggle switches for controlling the flash floodlight (14), record player (15), red light (16), and house lights (17).

The equipment used for the screens and rigging is typical stage construction type.

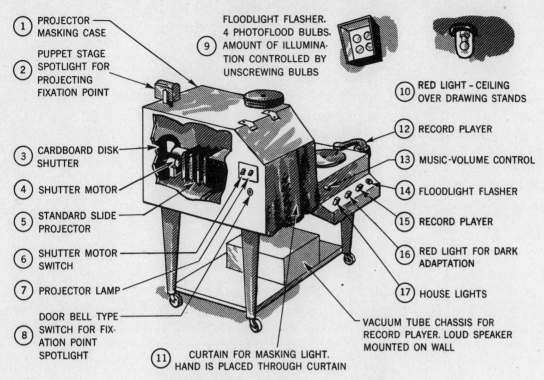

1. PROJECTOR MASKING CASE

2. PUPPET STAGE SPOTLIGHT FOR PROJECTING FIXATION POINT

3. CARDBOARD DISK SHUTTER

4. SHUTTER MOTOR

5. STANDARD SLIDE PROJECTOR

6. SHUTTER MOTOR SWITCH

7. PROJECTOR LAMP

8. DOOR BELL TYPE SWITCH FOR FIXATION POINT SPOTLIGHT

9. FLOODLIGHT FLASHER. 4 PHOTOFLOOD BULBS. AMOUNT OF ILLUMINATION CONTROLLED BY UNSCREWING BULBS

10. RED LIGHT - CEILING OVER DRAWING STANDS

11. CURTAIN FOR MASKING LIGHT. HAND IS PLACED THROUGH CURTAIN

12. RECORD PLAYER

13. MUSIC-VOLUME CONTROL

14. FLOODLIGHT FLASHER

15. RECORD PLAYER

16. RED LIGHT FOR DARK ADAPTATION

17. HOUSE LIGHTS

VACUUM TUBE CHASSIS FOR RECORD PLAYER. LOUD SPEAKER MOUNTED ON WALL

Figure 30. Projector and record player assembly.

Photographs in Figures 5 and 6 show the roll curtain, sandbagged spot lines, and pinrail. The spot lines are used on the flanking curtains and the three-dimensional models.

The present laboratory is being remodeled (Figure 31) to include several features which are desirable. The projector and record-playing equipment are to be placed on a bridge above and behind the students to·free floor space for more drawing stands and to allow more efficient floor projection. The space under the bridge is to be used for materials and as a convenient gathering point for the students during the intervals before drawing when their eyes are becoming dark-adapted.

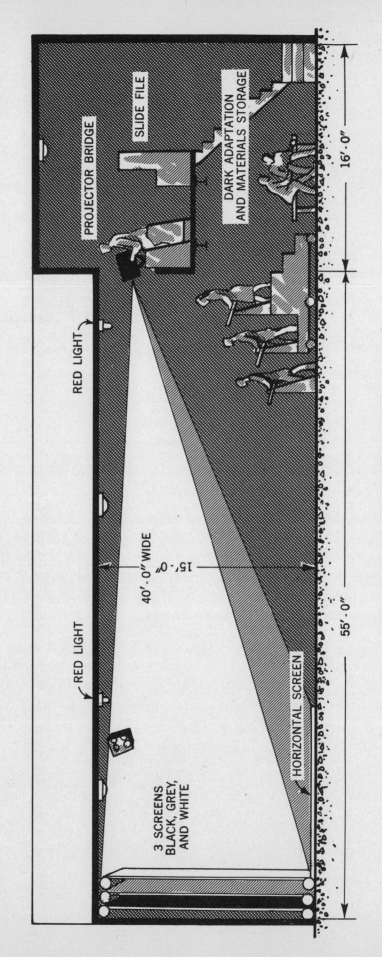

Figure 31. Cross section of laboratory under construction.

Appendix B

DESCRIPTION OF THE VISUAL TESTING EQUIPMENT AND PROCEDURE

T HIS DESCRIPTION of the visual testing equipment and procedures is for those investigators who want to undertake a program of visual tests similar to those used in this experiment. The problem is technical and requires a specialized knowledge of the field.

The Equipment

A large white screen, "A" in Figure 32, was prepared. It was illuminated by a bank of 40 W. lamps placed at "B" (Figure 32), 5' 4" from "A." The position for the lights was so chosen as to provide a uniform illumination over the surface of the screen from side to side. The lamps were below the subject's line of sight and were shielded so that only reflected light from the screen could reach the subject. The brightness half the way up the screen was 11.6 c/m^2.

The subject was seated at a small table bearing the head rest and light shielding arrangement shown in Figure 32. His position was such that a line perpendicular to the center of the screen would strike the mid-point of the line joining the pupils of his eyes. The distance from the eyes of the subject to the screen was six meters. The light shield in front of the subject allowed a complete view of the screen horizontally from either eye.

Behind the large screen was a long optical bench, parallel to the screen ("C" in Figure 32). At its center a mirror was mounted and rotated around a vertical axis to a position 45° from the axis of the optical bench. The mirror could be faced, at 45°, toward either end of the bench so that both ends might be used for testing.

At one end of the bench was located the central acuity measuring system ("D" in Figure 32, and "A" in Figure 34), consisting of a field lens, a movable lens, and a stationary target. The stationary target ("A" in Figure 35) consisted of a pair of black bars on a bright background. The subject was able to see an image of the target formed by lenses "F" and "M" and the mirror "R" (Figure 34) through a two-inch hole in a white cardboard mounted on the front of the white screen. The white background of the bars, inside the aperture, had the same brightness and color as the cardboard. The

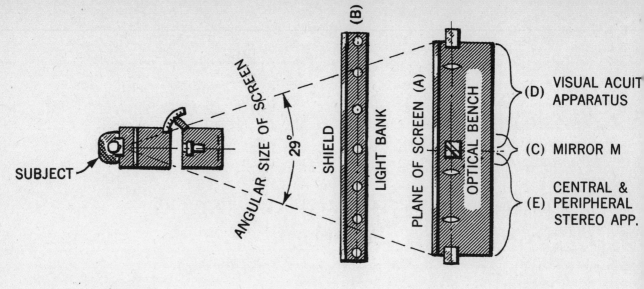

SUBJECT

ANGULAR SIZE OF SCREEN

29°

(B)

SHIELD

LIGHT BANK

PLANE OF SCREEN (A)

OPTICAL BENCH

(D) VISUAL ACUIT
APPARATUS

(C) MIRROR M

(E) CENTRAL &
PERIPHERAL
STEREO APP.

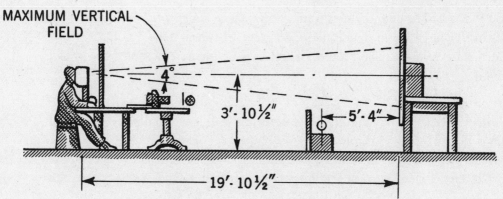

MAXIMUM VERTICAL
FIELD

4°

3'- 10½"

5'- 4"

19'- 10½"

Figure 32. General layout of subject and screen.

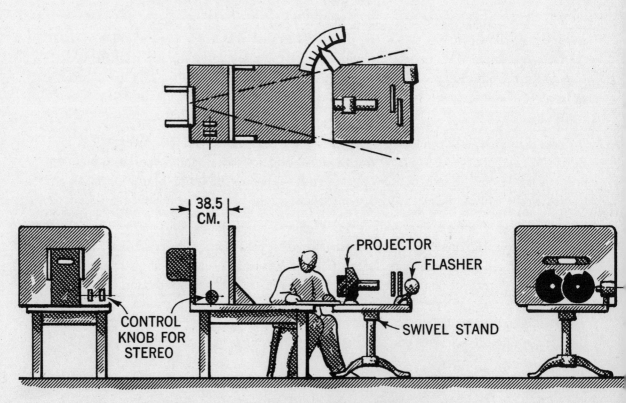

38.5
CM.

PROJECTOR

FLASHER

CONTROL
KNOB FOR
STEREO

SWIVEL STAND

Figure 33. Details showing screening arrangement around subject.

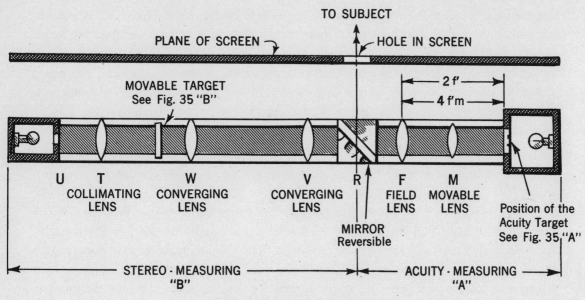

Figure 34. Details of optical bench.

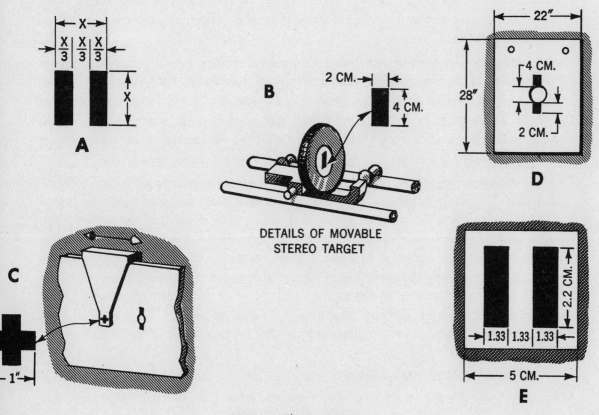

Figure 35. Details of target.

image of the target was made to diminish or enlarge by moving the lens "M" which was calibrated in terms of the Snellen Fraction. When "M" is half way between the target and the field lens, the image lies in the plane of the field lens. When "M" is either moved forward to decrease the image size or backward to increase the size, the image is slightly displaced in front of the field lens. However, allowance for this displacement of the image toward the subject is taken into account in calculating the Snellen Fraction. The focal length of the field lens (2f′) is twice that of the movable lens (f′m). The distance between the field lens and the target is 4 fm.

On the other end of the bench, the optical system was designed for measuring stereo-acuity ("E" in Figure 32, and "B" in Figure 34). The lenses "W" and "V" and the mirror "R" (Figure 34) form an image of the target which lies on the line "XX′" either in front or behind the plane of the screen, depending on the position of the target. For details of the target, see "B" in Figure 35. The subject could control the position of the target image by moving the target with a control knob on the table at which the subject sits (shown in Figure 33, in the side view). The optical system was designed to give the target image a constant angular size regardless of its distance in front or behind the plane of the screen. Mounted on the front of the screen was a white card ("E" in Figure 35) with a 3″ hole at its center and with black rectangles at the top and bottom. These rectangles have the same angular size as the target which the subject sees through the center of the aperture. The light source "U" (Figure 34) provides a bright background for the target so that the brightness of the area inside the aperture is equal to that of the white card.

For measuring peripheral stereo-acuity, a point of fixation (black cross "C" in Figure 35) was provided which could be placed at varying distances to the left of the center of the screen. The fixation point support was hooked over the upper edge of the white screen so that it could be moved. On its back side a pointer was made, and the screen painted with calibrated marks so that as the black cross was moved to left and right, its location could be noted from behind the screen during the stereo tests.

For measuring peripheral acuity a red fixation spot was provided in the center of the screen. The acuity target was momentarily flashed on the darkened screen by a projector and mechanical flasher mounted on a projector table in front of the subject. (See Figure 33.) Exposures were made at the rate of one every 7.5 seconds. The projector table was mounted on a pivot at its center so the position on the screen of the projected image could be silently changed. The projector table was provided with a pointer riding on a stationary scale attached to the adjacent table at which the subject sits. The scale was marked off into ten equal divisions encompassing a total of 28° arc. This provided for a projected target sweep of 14° on either side of the fixation point at the center of the screen.

The image used for the peripheral acuity target was photographically placed on a clear glass slide for use in the projector. One end of the glass had two vertical bars (as

72

shown in "D" Figure 35), and the other end, two similar horizontal bars. By sliding the glass in the projector, a shift could be made from one pair of bars to the other during the interim between flash exposures.

The target used for brightness discrimination was a simple circular spot produced by substituting in the projector a metal slide instead of the photographic bars. This metal slide had a circular window containing frosted glass. The image of this circular window, projected on the screen, constituted the target. The intensity of the projected target was controlled by an iris diaphragm accurately calibrated in one unit steps of area from 1 to 10. This diaphragm was mounted directly over the front of the projector within easy reach of the operator. The bank of 40 W. lamps was used in this test to illuminate the screen, giving a brightness value half way up the screen of 11.6 c/m^2. The brightness of the initial projected target was 0.4 c/m^2. The diameter of the projected target was 1°54′.

The Procedure

For testing central acuity, the subject was seated with his head pressed against the forehead rest. His head was so adjusted that he could see the entire screen from one side to the other, and his attention was fixed on the double bar target ("A" Figure 35) seen through a 2″ hole in the center of the screen. Starting with the target reduced to some sub-threshold value, the operator increased the size of the target. The subject was instructed to report as soon as he was able to perceive the double nature of the target, whether he actually saw two bars or just two spots. The operator endeavored to keep the rate of the size increase constant. A rough approximation of this rate is a change of two Snellen units per second (e.g., 20/15 to 20/17 in 1 sec.).

For the test of central stereo-acuity, the operator removed the 2″ aperture used in the central acuity test, and placed on the screen the reticle pattern shown in "E," Figure 34. Rotation of the mirror through 90° brought the stereopsis testing equipment on the optical bench into operation. The subject was then instructed to set the movable center bar on a plane with the two bars of the reticle pattern, using the control knob shown in the "side-view," Figure 33. The subject was allowed six attempts at setting the target on plane. Between each setting the central movable bar was blacked out for the subject while the operator repositioned the target for a new setting. The subject was permitted to move the target back and forth as much as he liked and to make the final movement from either direction, but the operator always pre-set the target half of the time in front and half of the time behind the reticle. If, during the subject's attempts to set the target on plane, he hit the limits of movement of the target, he was stopped and started over again.

The equipment for measuring peripheral stereo-acuity was the same as for central stereo-acuity except for the addition on the front of the screen of the movable fixation target ("C," Figure 35). The subject was instructed to observe this point while he set

73

the movable bar in the same plane as the reticle. Data were taken with the fixation target placed at successive intervals of 1° toward the periphery on the right side of the visual field either until the subject quit, or until his settings became so difficult to make that he frequently hit the stops.

The measurement of peripheral acuity required the use of the projector and mechanical flasher, plus a red fixation spot formed by placing a white card with 1 cm. square opening, covered with red gelatin in its center, on the screen in place of the stereopsis reticle. This hole was illuminated from behind. The room was thrown in darkness and the subject with one eye occluded was required to watch the red spot. At intervals of 7.5 seconds a momentary exposure of the acuity bars was made. The subject was shown how the position and orientation of the acuity target might be changed. He was further directed to guess if at any time he was not sure what had been flashed on the screen. A total of one hundred flash exposures were presented at random, ten exposures at each of ten different positions across the screen. These exposures were further modified by presenting the acuity bars vertically or horizontally in an independent random order.

The brightness discrimination test was conducted at night to insure total darkness in the testing room except for the field lights. This also helped assure that the illumination on the screen would be the same at all subsequent tests. The same projector and mechanical flasher were used for this experiment as in the peripheral acuity test, except for the addition to the projector of the iris diaphragm and the slide to produce the spot target projected on the screen.

The procedure in the brightness test was to present this low intensity spot on a bright uniform field while the subject fixated the red point in the center of the field. Eight degrees right and eight degrees left of the center of the screen were chosen as the two positions in which the spot might be presented. At various intensity levels of the spot, five rights and five lefts were presented in a predetermined random fashion. The subject was directed not to guess, but to say "right" or "left," depending on which side of the screen he saw the spot flashed. No response was given if he failed to see the target. Few wrong judgments were given, but these were treated as no judgments when they occurred. A few judgments which bore no relation to the timing of the exposures were disregarded. After ten exposures at the maximum brightness of the spot, its brightness was changed to 0.9 of the maximum without interruption of the exposures. After ten more exposures it was changed again to 0.8 of the maximum. This procedure was continued until the subject missed ten consecutive exposures. The test was so designed that the subject prior to training could no longer see the spot when it had reached approximately 50% of its maximum brightness.

Appendix C

CLARIFICATION OF CÉZANNE

THOSE WHO understand the principles of perceptual unity as evolved in the main body of the text will realize that a fresh approach to Cézanne is now possible. Many attempts have been made to explain Cézanne's words and works but have fallen short of their goal because of a failure to understand the role of perception in the arts. Cézanne was continually trying to make this point clear, as may be seen in the following quotations:

"In painting there are two factors, the eye and the brain, which must help each other, and we must work for their mutual development, with the eye by observing nature, with the brain through the study of the organized sensations which furnish the means of expression"[1]—direct recognition of the fact that the process of seeing is embedded in the process of painting.

"I mean that in an orange, an apple, a sphere, a head, there is a focal point, and this point is always the nearest to our eye, no matter how it is affected by light, shade, sensations of color"[2]—an exposition of three fundamental principles in his perception: (1) he sees a focal point; (2) this point is determined by its position in space relative to the

VANISHING POINT AT INFINITY

FOCAL POINT

Figure 36.

[1] Georges Rivière, *Paul Cézanne* (Paris: H. Floury, 1923), p. 137.
[2] Gerstle Mack, *Paul Cézanne* (New York: Alfred A. Knopf, 1935), p. 380.

75

observer; and (3) it is not affected by color or brightness, but is a function of position. Position is primary over color and brightness.

"The edges of objects recede toward a center located on our horizon"[3] — a way of saying that the periphery of forms in the motif are seen in relation to the vanishing point, and, in conjunction with his previous statement about the focal point, of saying that the vanishing point is an extension of the focal point through the visual field. Figure 36 illustrates how the vanishing point is an extension of the focal point through the visual field, perception being such as to organize all points or forms in the field in relation to the axis formed between the focal point and the vanishing point. This conception of organization must in no way be confused with geometrical perspective which is only a geometrical formula for controlling apparent diminution of size by the converging of contours at the vanishing point.

"It (the eye) becomes concentric through observation and work"[4]—an over-simplified way of saying that as the eye becomes trained in the way Cézanne was seeing, it comes to see concentrically, i.e. with the habit of relating peripheral forms in the field to a focal point. In Cézanne's unfinished studies, one sees the peripheral placement of color spots, with the focal area remaining as bare canvas. The center emerges through interrelations of peripheral points. Peripheral points, in Cézanne, are color spots, and his color modulations are effected in terms of concentric relations around the focal area, as are clearly apparent in his unfinished "La Route," illustrated in Figure 37.[5]

Figure 37.

"Here on the banks of the river the *motifs* are teeming, the same subject seen from a different angle suggests a subject of the highest interest, and so varied that I could keep myself busy for months without moving from one spot, just by leaning now to the right, now to the left"[6]— a vivid way of explaining that slight changes in the positional relations of forms in a visual field make entirely new motifs. It is the interrelation of points that makes the motif.

As these quotations suggest, Cézanne was extraordinarily aware of what was happening while he was painting. In hundreds of ways he tried to explain, involving himself in figures of speech which appear to the literal minded as a hopeless mass of contradictions and confusions. But both his words and his works become clear and consistent,

[3] *Ibid.*, p. 380.
[4] *Ibid.*, p. 380.
[5] From John Rewald, *Paul Cézanne, Correspondence* (Paris: Bernard Grasset, 1937).
[6] Mack, *op. cit.*, p. 389.

one with the other, when interpreted in terms of the principles of perceptual unity as a basis for understanding the graphic arts.[7] These principles, similarly applied to the works of other masters, both old and modern, bring clarity to the whole problem of visual form and the processes by which successful drawing and painting are achieved.[8]

Clearly Cézanne knew what he was trying to do and the role he was playing in the evolution of fresh conceptions of art forms and processes. A month before his death, he made the following statement:

"You will forgive me for harping constantly on the same string, but I am progressing towards the logical development of what we see and feel by studying nature; a consideration of processes comes later, processes being for us nothing but simple methods of making the public feel what we ourselves feel, and for making ourselves intelligible. The masters we admire can have done no more than that."[9]

He was taking as his job "progressing towards the logical development of what we see and feel by studying nature," and was fully aware that this was a basic job that had to be done before "processes" could be made clear. To others he was leaving the job of clarifying processes. This has been the main task of the present book; looking back, the processes of Cézanne and many other masters become clear.

---

[7] The diagrammatic analysis of Cézanne's composition as evolved by Erle Loran lead Loran to conclude that there is conflict between what Cézanne said about his procedures and what Cézanne actually did while painting. This is in sharp contrast to our own conclusion as to the consistency between Cézanne's explanations and his works. For Loran's case, see his *Cézanne's Composition* (Berkeley and Los Angeles; University of California Press, 1944).

Also in sharp contrast is a conclusion drawn by Barnes: "It is natural, therefore, that Cézanne's most characteristic compositional arrangement should be that of the most stable of all natural objects or architectural structures—the pyramid." See Albert C. Barnes and Violette De Mazia, *The Art of Cézanne* (New York; Harcourt Brace and Company, 1939), p. 44.

Both Loran and Barnes have mistaken some of the emergent effects in Cezanne's configuration for his basic structure.

[8] The author has recently completed in manuscript form an extensive study of many important drawings in terms of the principles of perceptual unity.

[9] Mack, *op. cit.*, p. 390.